60 MACHINE QUILTING PATTERNS

Pat Holly and Sue Nickels

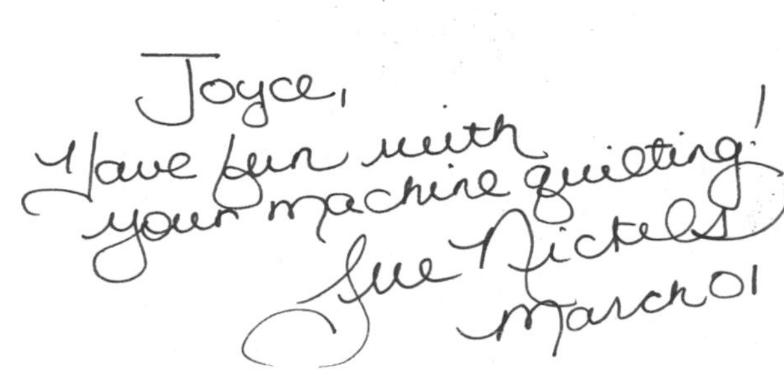

DOVER PUBLICATIONS, INC.
New York

INTRODUCTION

DURING THIS CURRENT quiltmaking revival, more and more quilts are being produced by more and more people with different needs. Many are drawn to this medium because of their love for the "old quilts." However, not everyone wants to, or can, take the time to reproduce one of these exquisite, but labor-intensive, heirlooms. By using the sewing machine, quilters can make the quilts they love in a smaller amount of time.

We have been machine quilting some of our quilts since 1988. Sue began teaching machine quilting then and has had enthusiastic response to all her classes since. We still love hand piecing and hand quilting, but, sometimes, time is limited and a quilt must be finished more quickly than hand quilting allows. Or, sometimes, a quilt is designed from start to finish to be made on the machine. We feel there is a place in the quilt world for both hand- and machine-made quilts. One is not "better" than the other, they are merely different choices for your quilt. Both take skilled hands. We think it is fun to make quilts that look like old quilts, but are made with modern technology.

After a quilt top has been completed you must decide how to quilt it. We feel, as do many others, that this part of making a quilt is just as important as designing the top. After all, quilting is what makes a quilt a quilt! There are many pattern books available with wonderful designs; however, we saw the need for some designs made specifically for the machine quilter. Our inspiration has often been old quilts. We decided to look at as many old quilts as we could and adapt the quilting designs for the machine. This is something you can do, too! Look at old quilts, photos of old quilts and anything else you can find, and examine the quilting. Once you start doing this, you will be amazed at the number of different ideas you find, sometimes on the same quilt. And don't look just at the quilting—many beautiful appliqué patterns also work well as quilting designs.

The General Instructions section will help you get started. This presents the method Sue teaches in her classes. It is not meant to be a complete course on how to do machine quilting. There are many thorough books covering the subject and we urge you to look at them or to take a class. Machine quilting is not just simple, straight lines! The free-motion technique does require practice, but if you practice, practice, practice, you will be pleased with the result.

In this book, we hope you will find quilting designs to use as is for your quilts or to serve as inspiration for new designs. Try combining some of these designs, look at old quilts for ideas or simply use your imagination! Beautiful quilts of heirloom quality can be made using your sewing machine.

This book is dedicated to our mother and father, Tiny and Jerry Holly, because they are always there to support and encourage our creativity.

Thank you to Ann Augustin for proofreading.

Published in Canada by General Publishing Company, Ltd., 30 Lesmill Road, Don Mills, Toronto, Ontario.

Bibliographical Note

60 Machine Quilting Patterns is a new work, first published by Dover Publications, Inc., in 1994.

Library of Congress Cataloging-in-Publication Data

Holly, Pat.
60 machine quilting patterns / Pat Holly and Sue Nickels.
p. cm.
ISBN 0-486-28013-6
1. Machine quilting—Patterns. I. Nickels, Sue. II. Title. III. Title: Sixty machine quilting patterns.
TT835.H556 1994
746.9'7041—dc20 93-50914
CIP

Manufactured in the United States of America
Dover Publications, Inc., 31 East 2nd Street, Mineola, N.Y. 11501

GENERAL INSTRUCTIONS

Supplies Used

Sewing Machine

A sewing machine is the essential supply for machine quilting. Any sewing machine can do quilting, although some machines can only quilt straight lines. For free-motion quilting, you need a darning foot and the ability to lower or cover the feed dogs of your machine. Some of the newer, more complex machines make the job of machine quilting easier, but don't despair—most machines can be used if you have the patience to make appropriate adjustments. Remember to keep your sewing machine in good working condition and to clean and oil it regularly.

Walking or Even-Feed Foot

A walking foot (also called an even-feed foot) is used to quilt straight lines. The walking foot acts like a top set of feed dogs, feeding all layers of the quilt through the machine evenly, preventing puckering or shifting of layers. If you do not have a walking foot, you can use a regular foot, but you may experience some shifting of the layers as you quilt.

Darning Foot

A darning foot is essential for free-motion quilting. The feed dogs must be lowered or covered, depending on your sewing machine. This technique enables you to do all those wonderful traditional quilting designs like feathers or hearts. Free-motion quilting feels very different from regular sewing and can be described as drawing with your sewing machine. A darning foot was probably not included with your sewing machine and will have to be purchased from your sewing machine dealer.

Thread

We use transparent nylon thread, often sold in quilt shops specifically for machine quilting, for the top of most of our machine-quilted quilts. YLI and Clotilde are examples of brand names. The size is described as ".004." We like the transparency of the nylon thread—it can be used over all colors of fabrics, so there is no need to change thread colors. We also like the softness of the thread, as it gives the feel of a hand-quilted quilt. One disadvantage of this thread is that it is slightly heat sensitive. You cannot iron with a hot iron directly on a quilt top. However, we do not iron our quilts after they are quilted. If you do not want to use nylon thread, regular sewing thread can be used on the top of the quilt. We do not use the nylon thread in the bobbin; instead we use 50-weight 100% cotton thread. Use a color that is complementary to the quilt top. We find that the combination of the two threads (nylon on top/cotton in the bobbin) gives the feel we want in our quilts. You can experiment with other threads to find what best suits your project.

Caution: Dispose of nylon thread clippings carefully. Pets might pick the threads off the floor, swallow them and be injured.

Sewing Machine Needles

80/12 is the preferred needle size for machine quilting.

Safety Pins

We like to use size 0 or 1 brass safety pins to baste our quilts for machine quilting. Pin basting works better than thread basting. With machine quilting, you are sewing lots of very small stitches over the basting threads, making the threads difficult to remove. With pin basting, just remove the pins as you get to them while you are sewing.

Batting

There are many different battings available for machine quilting. In keeping with our love of a traditional look to our quilts, we use cotton batting. We have also found it somewhat easier to quilt with cotton batting as opposed to polyester batting. Mountain Mist "Blue Ribbon" batting is an excellent choice for machine quilting. With this type of batt, you must quilt every 1½" to 2". "Heirloom" cotton batting by Hobbs is another excellent batting for the machine, and quilting may be spaced every 3" or less.

Polyester batts can also be used in machine quilting. They are more "slippery" than cotton batts, therefore you need to baste closer together. When using polyester, choose low or traditional loft—high-loft polyester batts are meant for comforters and can be very difficult to machine quilt.

Markers

We use Berol Veri-thin marking pencils to mark the quilting designs on our quilts. Silver works for most fabrics; white works well on dark colors. If you do not mark too hard, the lines come off easily. They will either wear off over time or wash out when the quilt is laundered. If you have a particularly stubborn line, use a fabric eraser to remove it. There are many marking pencils and pens on the market. Always test your marking tool before you mark your entire quilt. One good way to test is to make a small, practice piece. Mark the quilting lines with several tools you want to try and use this to practice your machine quilting. Launder the piece the same way you plan to launder your quilt and see if the lines disappear.

Rubber Glove "Fingers"

When doing free-motion quilting, control of the quilt is very important. Sue likes to use fingertips (knuckle length) cut from rubber kitchen gloves to help grip the quilt. Use them on the thumb and first two fingers of both hands. Experiment and see if it helps. You can also use secretary's "fingers," available at office supply stores.

Preparing Your Quilt for Machine Quilting

Marking

We mark our quilt top before it is basted. Choose how you are going to quilt your quilt. Some straight lines may not need to be marked if they follow the piecing of the quilt, or are quilted "in the ditch" (exactly along a seam line). However, other straight lines, like diagonals or cross-hatching, may need marking. To mark straight lines, we use a quilter's ruler marked with inches, a 45° line and other necessary measurements.

To use the designs in this book, simply remove the appropriate page. If you prefer to keep the book intact, you can trace or photocopy the design. If you photocopy the design, you can also change the size as needed. Here are some different techniques for transferring the designs to your quilt top.

Light-colored fabrics: The designs can simply be traced by placing the design under the quilt top.

Dark or print fabrics: Since you cannot easily see through these fabrics to trace the design, there are two ways to put the quilting design on your quilt top.

Using a light box: Tape the design to the light box. Place your quilt top on the box and trace.

Making a template: You can use lightweight cardboard, template plastic or Mylar plastic film. For a cardboard template, transfer the design to the cardboard using carbon paper or simply glue the design to the cardboard. Cut your shape with scissors or an X-acto knife. For inside lines, cut thin slots. If using template plastic, lay the plastic over the quilting design and trace. Cut slots for the lines of the design with an X-acto knife, leaving connecting plastic so that the template does not fall apart. For Mylar plastic, trace the design as for template plastic. Make slots using an electric hot pen. Cut the slots for the lines leaving connecting plastic. Follow the directions that come with the hot pen.

For all methods of marking remember to use a sharp pencil and to mark lightly. You want to be able to see the designs, but the lines should be removable.

Basting

A well-basted quilt is very important to the success of machine quilting. Please take the time to do a good job with this sometimes tedious part of the quiltmaking process. The best way to baste a quilt is to stretch it in a full-sized frame and pin-baste. However, not all of us have the luxury of a full-sized frame. The following method is the next best way to pin-baste a quilt.

We always cut the backing and batting at least 2″ larger than the quilt top. Mark the center of each side of both the backing and the quilt top. This will allow you to line up your quilt accurately. Lay your quilt backing, wrong side up, either on a large table or on the floor. Using masking tape, tape the sides of the backing to the table or floor, stretching the backing slightly. If you are basting on a carpeted floor, you can use straight pins to secure the backing to the carpet. Lay your batting on the backing, smoothing out any fullness or wrinkles. Remove any threads that may cling to the batting. Next, place your pressed and marked quilt top right side up on the batting, matching your center marks so that the top and bottom are lined up. Smooth the quilt top, but do not stretch it or you may distort the piecing or appliqué. You are now ready to pin-baste *(Fig. 1)*.

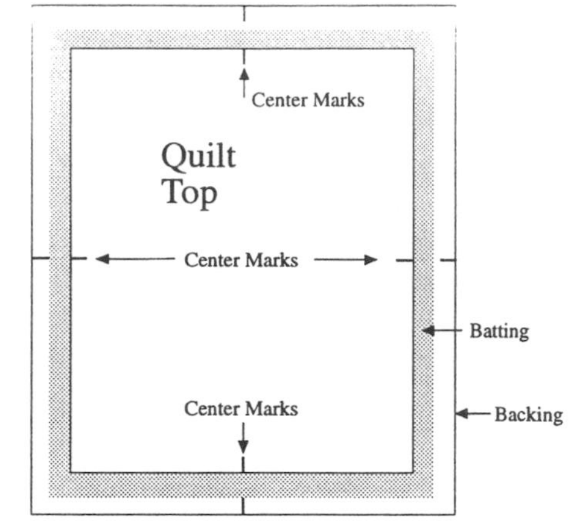

Fig. 1. Ready to baste.

We use size 0 or 1 brass safety pins. For cotton batting, pin every 4″; for polyester batting, you will need to pin every 3″. Starting in the center of the quilt, place pins out to the edge in the order shown in *Fig. 2.* Leave the pins open and close them when all the pins are in the quilt. The process of closing the safety pins can pull the backing and cause puckers. Place pins from the center diagonally out to the corners. Fill in the remaining areas with the proper amount of pins. You can now remove the tape from the backing and close all the safety pins. This is a finger-breaking job. A new tool called a Pin-Popper or Kwik-Klip helps with this chore.

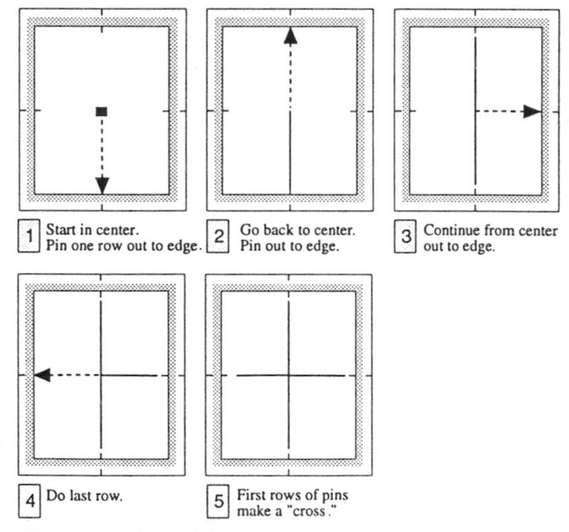

Fig. 2. Order of first pin placement.

If you are pinning on the floor, you may wish to move your quilt package carefully to a table in order to complete the basting, after you have pinned the rows shown in *Fig. 2.* Work on one quarter of the quilt at a time and carefully readjust the backing, batting and top.

After the pins are closed, hand baste the outside edge of your quilt top to the batting and backing. This, along with your 2″ extra backing, extends your quilt and makes it possible to free-motion quilt your border. We are now ready for machine quilting.

Machine Set-up

Bobbin: Fill the bobbin with 50-weight, 100% cotton thread. Select a color to blend with the quilt top and backing. For the backing fabric, choose a color that goes with the quilt top. A small print works well to camouflage any stitch irregularities that can show up on the back of the quilt. If your bobbin thread contrasts with the quilt top, you may see the bobbin thread showing on the top of the quilt.

Nylon Thread: Proper threading of the nylon thread is one of the most important steps in successful machine quilting. Nylon thread is very fine. If you thread as you usually do (with the spool on the spool holder), the turning of the spool will cause the top tension to become too tight. The spool of nylon thread must be taken off the spool holder and placed behind the machine and close to it *(Fig. 3)*. An empty bobbin (with holes) placed on the regular spool holder can serve as an extra thread guide. Taking the spool off the machine allows the nylon thread to come off the spool smoothly with no tension. Sometimes the thread comes off the spool too fast and causes curls that can get caught and break the

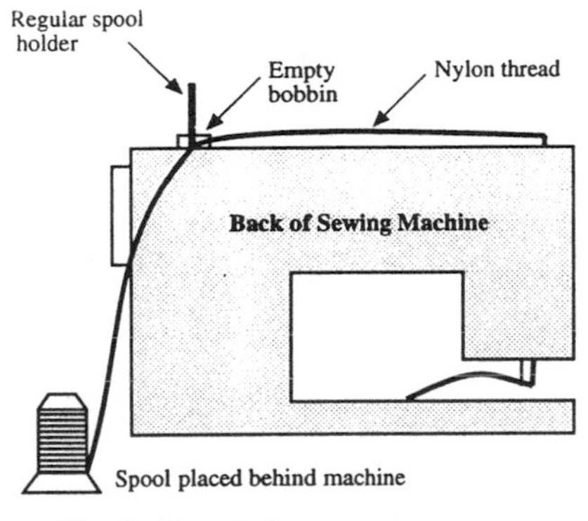

Fig. 3. Spool placement.

thread. If this happens, you can use a thread sock or net (available for serger thread) and place it over the nylon thread. This will slow the thread release slightly. Machines with horizontal spool holders may work fine as intended, but if the thread catches and breaks frequently, use the method just described.

Use a size 80/12 needle in your machine and you are ready to machine quilt.

Different Types of Machine Quilting

Straight-Line Quilting

Use a walking foot for quilting straight lines, so that the quilt layers feed evenly through the machine. To secure threads for straight stitching, hold the nylon thread and take one stitch manually (down and up once with the needle). Raise the walking foot and pull the bobbin thread to the top. This allows you to hold the threads as you start sewing and prevents the threads from jamming the machine. *Always know where your threads are!* Set your stitch-length control for very small stitches; start sewing, then gradually increase the stitch length until you reach the regular stitch length. From where you start stitching to the point you reach the regular stitch length should measure about ¼". There should be at least 8–12 very small stitches securing the threads. The thread ends (nylon and bobbin) can now be clipped. Continue straight stitching, following your marked line carefully. The walking foot will feed the quilt evenly from the top, matching the feed of the feed dogs on the bottom. If you are using a regular presser foot, place your hands on either side of the presser foot and gently help the layers of the quilt feed evenly. Never pull the quilt from in front and behind the presser foot, as this will stretch the row of stitching and distort your quilt.

Stitch length for straight stitching is usually between 10–14 stitches per inch. This is between 2–3 on the stitch length indicator for most machines. If the stitches are too large, the nylon threads may catch on things; if they are too small, they will not resemble hand quilting. Personal preference will determine what works best for you. To end your row of stitching, gradually decrease the stitch length to very small stitches, allowing ¼" as at the beginning of the row to end at the proper place. Clip the nylon thread from the top and the bobbin thread from the back of the quilt.

Free-Motion Quilting

Free-motion quilting enables you to do curved designs on the sewing machine. Place the darning foot on the machine and lower the feed dogs. On some machines the feed dogs cannot be lowered; instead, a cover is provided to stop the feed-dog motion from feeding fabric through. To begin, hold the nylon thread and take one stitch manually (down and up with the needle). Lift up the darning foot and pull the bobbin thread to the top. To secure the stitching, take small stitches, gradually getting larger, for about ¼". Clip the thread ends when you are far enough away to do so. Once the feed dogs are lowered (or covered) on your machine, you have no stitch-length control. You control the length of the stitches by moving the quilt. This is like drawing with your machine needle on your quilt. Start very slowly; move your hands and you will make the small stitches needed to secure the threads. When ending the stitching, you also need to take small stitches to secure the threads. Clip the threads on the top and back of the quilt.

Free-motion quilting is a wonderful technique that takes patience and practice to master. Because you control the stitch length by moving the quilt, it will take time to learn how to maintain a constant stitch size. The faster you move your hands, the larger your stitches; the slower you move your hands, the smaller the stitches.

The speed at which your machine runs also makes a difference in free-motion quilting. Sewing at a very slow speed makes it harder to control your stitching. A medium or medium-high speed seems to work well. The combination of how fast your machine runs and how fast you move your quilt is the formula needed to create a consistent stitch length.

The most important word in free-motion quilting is control. Here are some ideas to help you maintain control while quilting.

• Try not to lift your hands from your work as you sew. Stop sewing with your needle in the down position in the quilt, then reposition your hands. When you lift your hands as you quilt, you lose control and get uneven stitches.

• Think of free-motion quilting as you would think of driving a car—watch the road ahead of you (your design line), not the wheel of the car (the darning foot and needle).

• Use your whole upper body (hands, arms, shoulders) to control your stitching, not just your fingers.

• Use rubber glove fingers to help control and grip the quilt.

• Remember—practice, practice, practice makes you a better free-motion machine quilter!

Practice Samples

To get started with machine quilting, try working on three or four practice samples to familiarize yourself with the techniques. Use 10″ by 10″ squares of muslin, layered with batting and backing.

Start with straight stitching. Set up the machine as described above. Mark a grid on your muslin and layer with batting and backing, using safety pins to baste. The order of sewing for your square is the same as you would use for a large quilt. Start in the center at the top; stitch a line and move one line at a time to the right. This means you will only have half or less than half of the quilt under the arm of your machine. The bulk of the quilt is always moving to the left.

Start with the center row in the grid at the top of the piece. Secure the stitching and sew to the end of the row, removing safety pins as needed. Secure the stitching at the end. For the next row of stitching, move to the right (*Fig. 4*). Continue until all rows to the right of

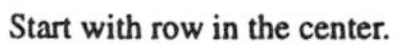

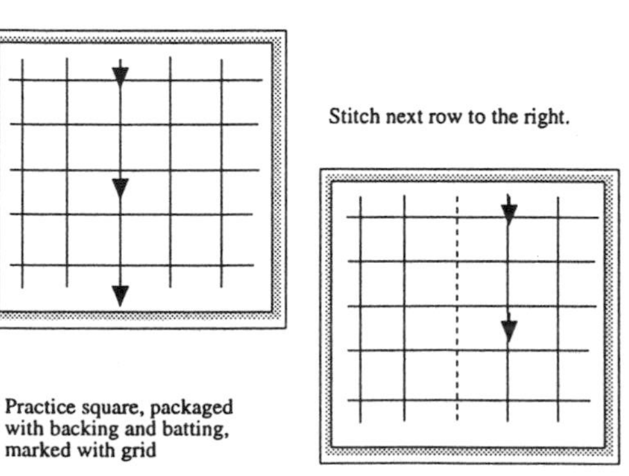

Fig. 4. Stitching order.

center are complete. Turn the square 180°; start again with the centermost row and sew the quilt from the center top to the right. Turn the square 90°; starting with the center row, stitch rows moving to the right. Turn the square 180°; begin with the centermost row and finish your practice square. Check the tension of your stitching. Look for any puckers, folds or shifting on the top or bottom. This will indicate how your machine is feeding the layers through as you sew. If you are having problems, review the section on straight-line quilting or look under "Problem Solving" (below).

Once you are happy with the result, you are ready to quilt straight lines on your quilt.

Practice free-motion quilting with another practice square. Use a plain square of muslin, batting and backing; baste with safety pins. Set up the machine as described in "Free-Motion Quilting." Start anywhere on the square; secure the threads and clip. Begin to play with the stitching. Do loops, circles, writing, etc. to become comfortable with your machine (*Fig. 5*). Remove safety pins as needed. Check for proper tension.

Fig. 5. Free-motion practice.

Some machines need adjusting when using nylon thread. If loops of bobbin thread show on top of the quilt, your top tension is too tight. Loosen it by moving the tension control to a smaller number. Make small adjustments, sew and check again. It may even be necessary to adjust your bobbin tension slightly on some machines. To tighten, turn the screw on the bobbin case slightly to the right (clockwise). Remember, righty-tighty, lefty-loosey.

Fig. 6. Stipple quilting.

Next practice some stipple quilting (*Fig.6*). Stipple quilting is a free-form, meandering line that can be used to fill a background area on your quilt. This is a fun and easy way to free-motion quilt. Stippling is made by sewing small circular loops that do not cross over each other. One way to think of the line is like little puzzle pieces. There is no perfect way to stipple. Like handwriting, everyone's stipple quilting will be different. Remember to always secure threads when starting and stopping.

You can now move on to practice designs. Trace a few patterns from this book onto a muslin square. Layer batting and backing; baste with safety pins. Trying to follow a marked line with free-motion quilting the first time can be a challenge. When following your marked design, think of it as a guideline. If you get off the line slightly, gradually move back until you are following the line again. Once the marked lines are removed, you will never know you were off by that slight amount.

Start at the top of your design and sew down. Always refer to the small diagrams given with the quilt pattern for the order of sewing. Remember how important control is and use the information given above to help maintain control. We have found that starting at the top of the design, stitching down, then starting again at the top seems to work best *(Fig. 7)*. You can move backwards up a design, but it is harder to control and difficult to see the lines because the darning foot blocks your view. You can do straight-line stitching with a darning foot, but it takes a lot of control to keep the stitches straight and even.

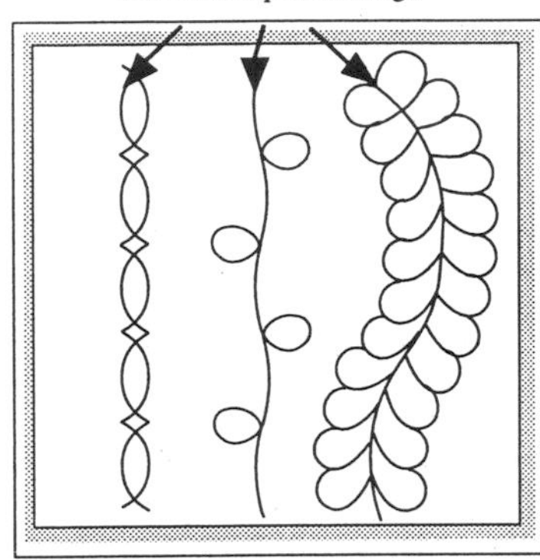

Fig. 7. Order of sewing.

Once you feel comfortable with your practice samples, it is time to quilt your quilt. Don't practice forever—everyone has to start their first quilt sometime!

Quilting Your Quilt

Choosing the Order of Machine Quilting

Once your quilt is marked, layered and basted, it is time to decide the order of machine quilting. We like to start with any straight-line stitching first. This helps to stabilize the quilt during the quilting process. Plan to start in the center of the quilt at the top and remember to always work from the center to the right. Stitch as much straight-line quilting as possible before switching to free-motion quilting. Keep practice samples around and, before you begin the free-motion stitching on your quilt, do a bit of sewing to refresh yourself on the technique (or vice versa, when going from free-motion to straight lines). If there are any problems or tension adjustments necessary, they will happen on the practice piece and not on your quilt. Try to avoid switching between the two types of quilting too often. You will probably need to quilt the inner portion of your quilt first, then the borders. Once you have planned your quilting order, it is time for the next step.

Packaging

Packaging your quilt for machine quilting is very important. In order to have good control of your quilt, whatever its size, you must package it properly. Lay your quilt on an area large enough to spread the entire quilt flat. Roll the quilt evenly from each side so that the roll is a few inches from your quilting line on either side. You may want to use quilter's bicycle clips to hold the rolls closed (polyester batting, in particular, tends to spring open). For a large quilt, roll tightly, so it will all fit under the arm of the machine. Then roll (or fan-fold back and forth) from the bottom of the quilt to the top, so it is easy to transport to the sewing area *(Fig. 8)*.

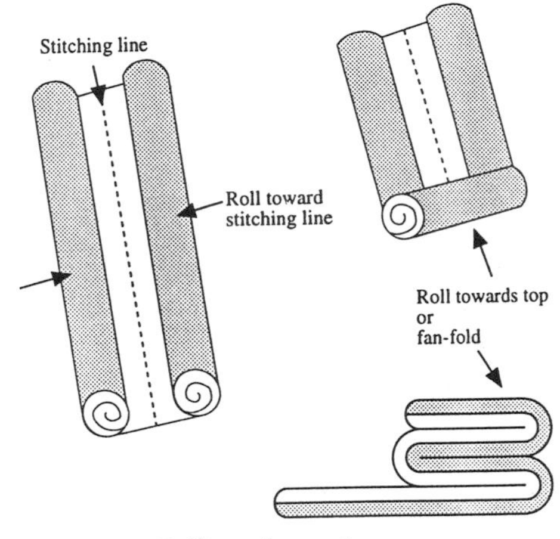

Fig. 8. Rolling the quilt.

Once at your sewing machine, place the quilt in the machine and set the roll against your chest or over your shoulder to support the weight of the quilt. Sew the row and continue moving to the right. Repackage as needed to complete the quilt. A large quilt needs to be repackaged often, as it will get out of control easily. For borders, roll the entire quilt from the left and work on one border at a time *(Fig. 9)*. For a review of quilting order, see the section "Practice Samples."

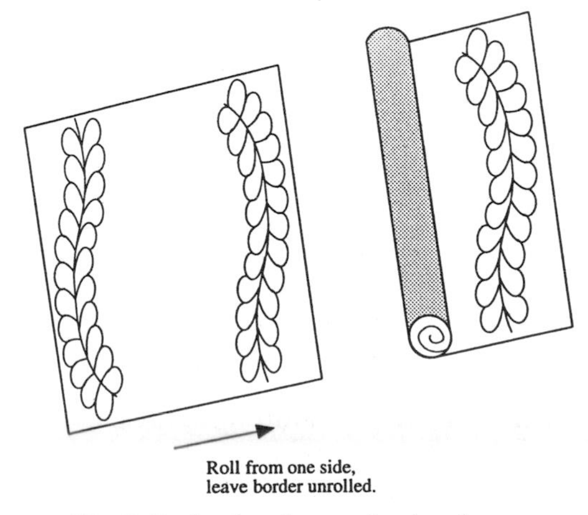

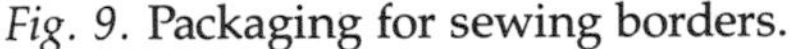

Fig. 9. Packaging for sewing borders.

When quilting a large quilt, you may need to put a chair behind you to support the quilt as it is draped over your shoulder. Remember that if your quilt unrolls and drops off the sewing table, this will pull on the quilt and cause you to lose control.

Repackage often to keep good control of your quilt. For quilts marked on the diagonal, package from the corners to the middle *(Fig. 10)*.

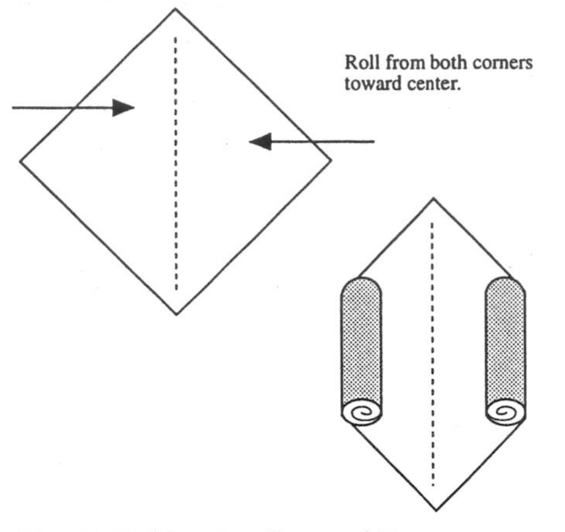

Fig. 10. Rolling for diagonal lines.

Your Workspace

Do not place your sewing machine table against a wall. The quilt will stop when it hits the wall, making quilting difficult. Always keep the work area clean of items that the quilt might push off the table. Ideally, your sewing machine should be at tabletop height. If your machine is too high, use a chair that brings you up higher, so that your arms are even with the machine.

When you have finished quilting, bind your quilt using your favorite method. We most often use a double bias binding, machine-sewn to the front of the quilt, brought to the back, then slip-stitched by hand. You could baste the binding to the back, then machine sew the binding close to the edge from the top of the quilt for a completely machine-made quilt!

Thread Options

Decorative threads such as metallics, rayons, silks and cottons can be used to machine quilt your quilt. Metallic thread sometimes breaks easily when machine quilting. Try using a 90/14 stretch needle. The larger opening and special coating make it easier for the thread to slide through the eye. New embroidery needles are also available. A lubricant called *Sewer's Aide* can be drizzled down along the side of the spool of thread (three stripes equally spaced), cutting down on the friction created by the thread passing through the needle's eye.

Because decorative threads can fray, don't clip the threads close to the quilt as you do when using nylon thread. Instead, leave a 5" tail of thread and secure with small stitches as described above. End with small stitches and leave another 5" tail of thread. After sewing, weave the thread tails between the quilt layers into the batting.

Rayon threads work beautifully for machine quilting. Use the 90/14 regular needle.

If you do not want to use decorative threads, but do not want to use nylon thread in your quilt either, regular sewing thread or cotton thread, in either 50- or 60-weight (a finer, but not as strong, thread), works well. Try to match the background fabric if you want to camouflage your stitching. Remember, all of these threads can be seen more clearly than nylon thread, so your stitching needs to be consistent and smooth. Using decorative threads can add variety and interest to your quilts but, for the beginner, nylon thread is a good choice.

Problem Solving

Reread all instructions for reminders on important information.

• If your nylon thread is breaking, take it out of your machine and rethread completely. This is the most common problem and is easily solved. Check to see that your spool has not fallen over and that the thread has not become caught on something. Next, rethread your bobbin and make sure there are no threads caught in the bobbin area. Nylon thread is very fine and can be hard to see. Check for any small pieces that may have fallen into the bobbin area and are caught in any of the metal parts. Most thread problems will be corrected by these measures.

• Clean and oil your machine regularly. Machine quilting is hard on your machine—treat it kindly!

• Dull or damaged sewing-machine needles can cause problems. Change your needle periodically.

• Take breaks often, particularly when working on a large quilt. Quilts are heavy and can tire you out. Get up and walk around. When you come back, you will be ready to continue!

Tension problems:

• If there are bobbin thread loops showing on the top of your quilt, your top tension is too tight. Loosen it by moving your top-tension control to a smaller number. If loosening the top tension does not seem to help, you may also need to tighten the bobbin tension. To tighten the bobbin tension, find the small screw on your bobbin holder and note its position (like the setting on a clock—2:00, 3:00, etc.). Turn the screw slightly to the right (clockwise). Do not make large changes; instead, make small adjustments, test, and if needed, make further changes. Some machines (like the Bernina) have a small hole or hook on the bobbin case. If you place the bobbin thread through the hole (see your instruction book), the bobbin tension will increase slightly.

• Some tension problems can be solved by using a straight-stitch throat plate. The layers of the quilt can be pulled down into the opening of a zigzag plate and cause problems with the stitch quality on the back of the quilt.

• Make sure you are using a good quality thread in your bobbin. 50-weight, 100% cotton works best. Cheap thread can cause tension problems.

• Be kind to yourself! Machine quilters tend to be very critical of themselves as they are quilting. You are doing a great job. When your quilt is finished, stand back and pat yourself on the back for a job well done!

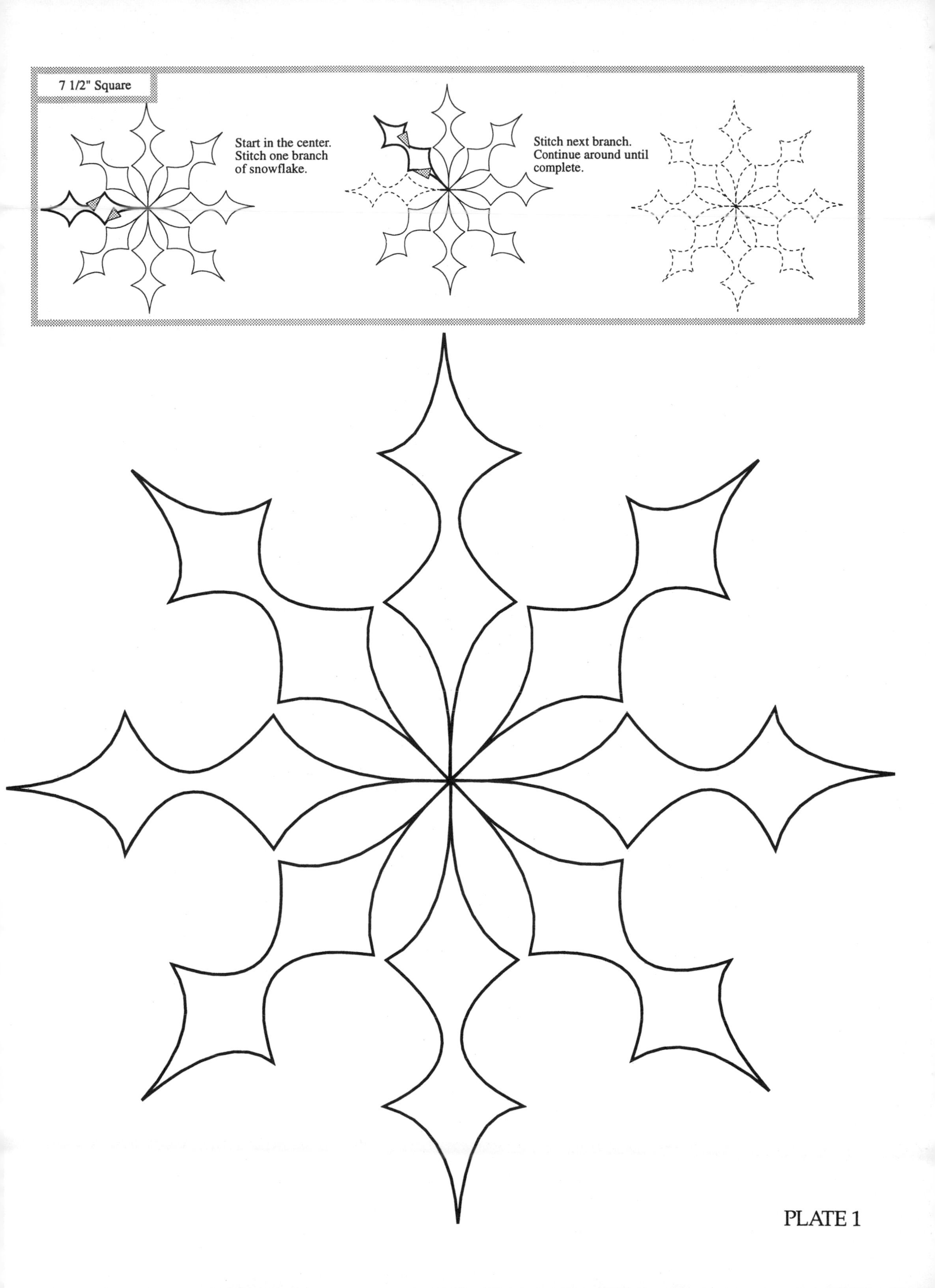
7 1/2" Square
Start in the center.
Stitch one branch
of snowflake.
Stitch next branch.
Continue around until
complete.
PLATE 1

7" Square
Start in center,
stitch inner loop.
Stitch larger loops.
Stitch last round of loops.

PLATE 2

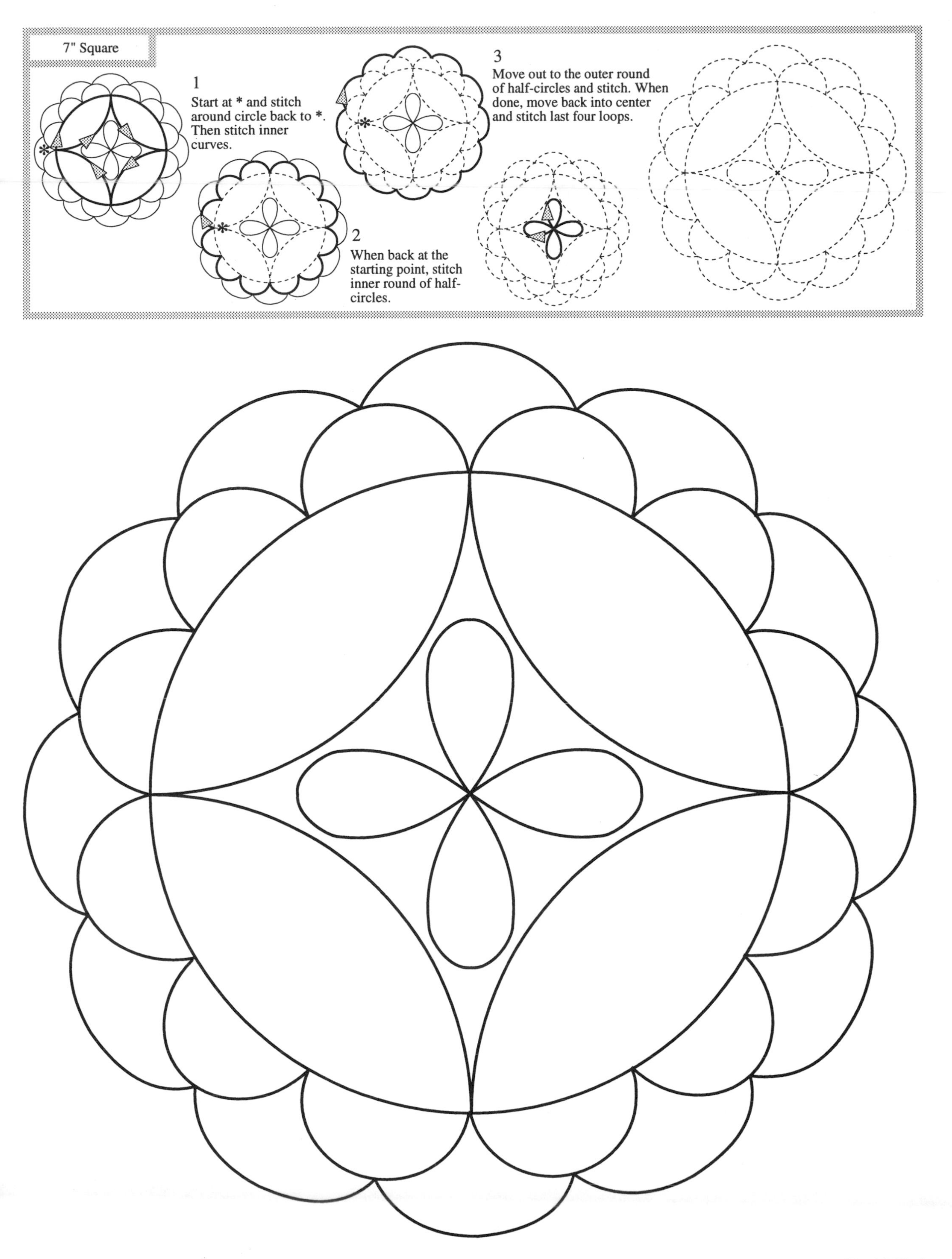
7" Square
1
Start at * and stitch around circle back to *. Then stitch inner curves.
2
When back at the starting point, stitch inner round of half-circles.
3
Move out to the outer round of half-circles and stitch. When done, move back into center and stitch last four loops.

PLATE 3

7" Square
Start in center. Stitch up one side and down the other.
Complete one segment. Stitch around the next three to complete design.

PLATE 4

7" Square
Start at center. Stitch back and forth along line to complete one branch. Repeat around to complete design.

PLATE 5

7" Square
Start in center at base of one branch. Stitch around leaves back to center. Continue around other three branches.

7" Square
Start at center and stitch up one side of flower. Stitch back down the other side and repeat for remaining three flowers.

PLATE 7

12" Square
One-quarter of design is given.

7" Square
Start with little hearts and curve.
Next, stitch big heart and loops.

5" Square
Stitch around inner part of hearts.
Stitch outer half of hearts.
2 1/4" High, 1 1/2" Repeat

5" High, 10" Long
Start at bottom, stitch four loops.
Go up to top and stitch five loops.
Move back to bottom and stitch last four loops.
4" High, 4" Wide

PLATE 11

2" High, 1 1/2" Repeat
Do one side first, then go back and do the other side.
2 1/4" High, 1" Repeat
Start at midpoint
Repeat on other side

PLATE 12

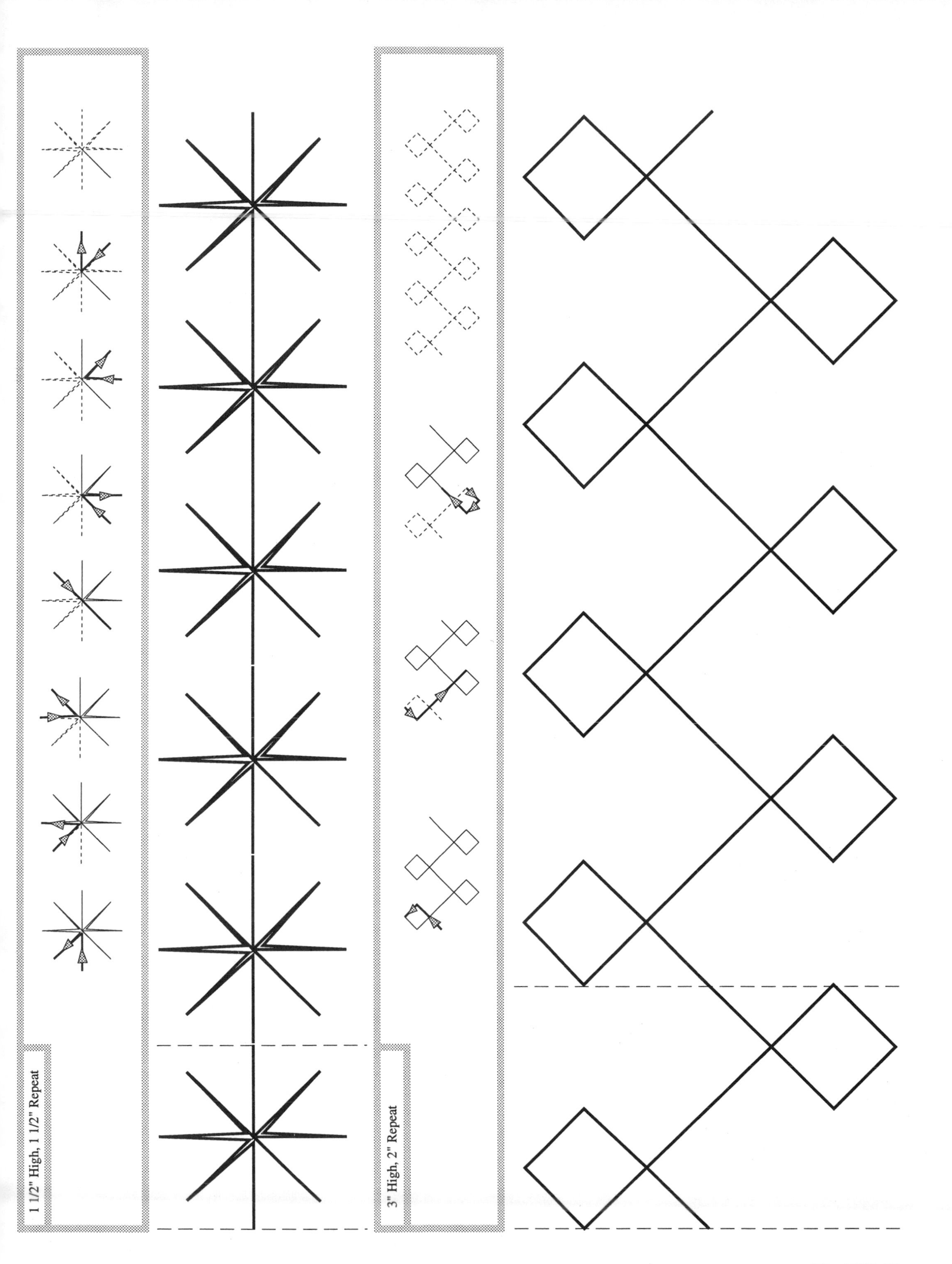

PLATE 13

PLATE 14

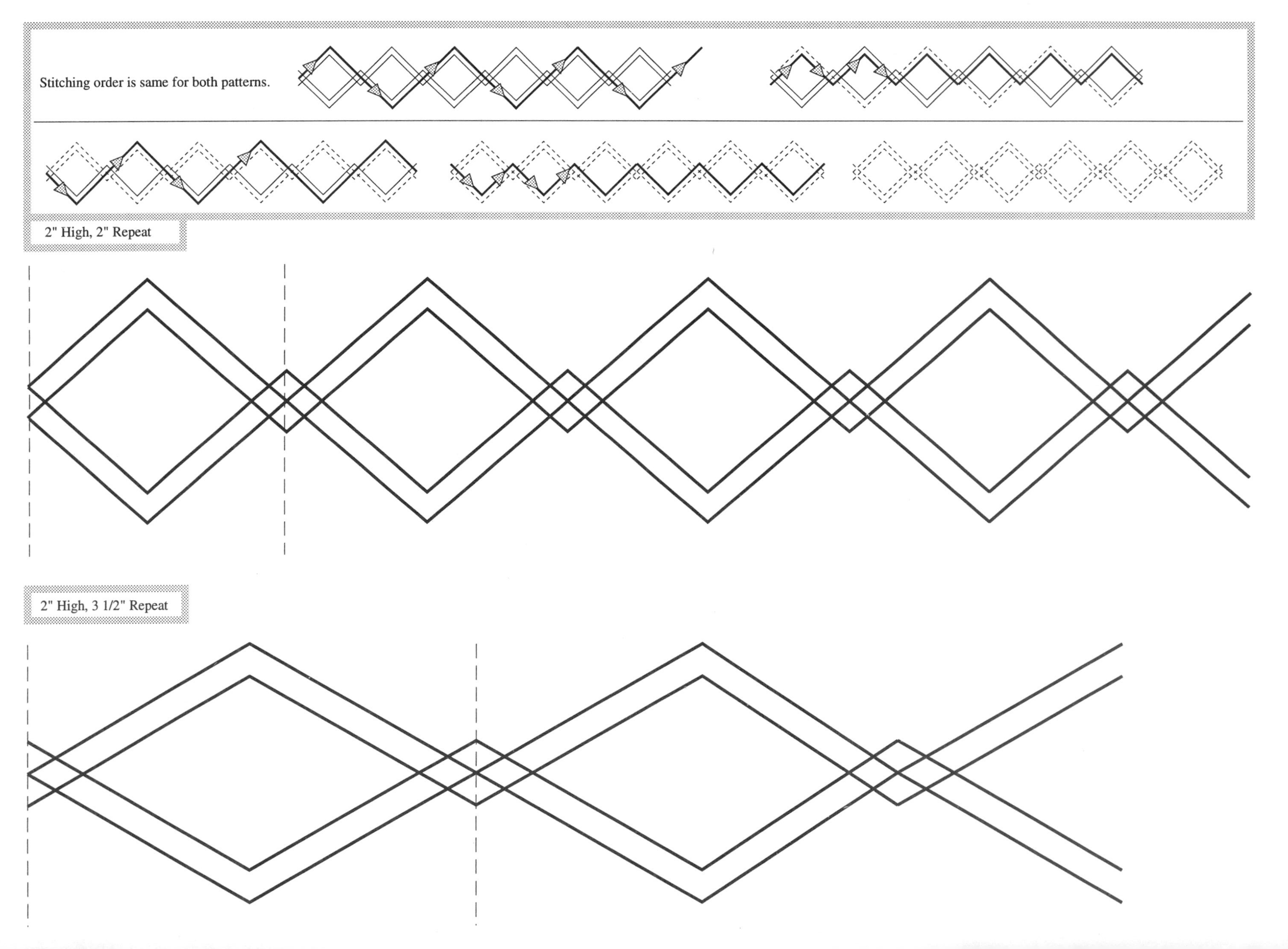
Stitching order is same for both patterns.
2" High, 2" Repeat
2" High, 3 1/2" Repeat

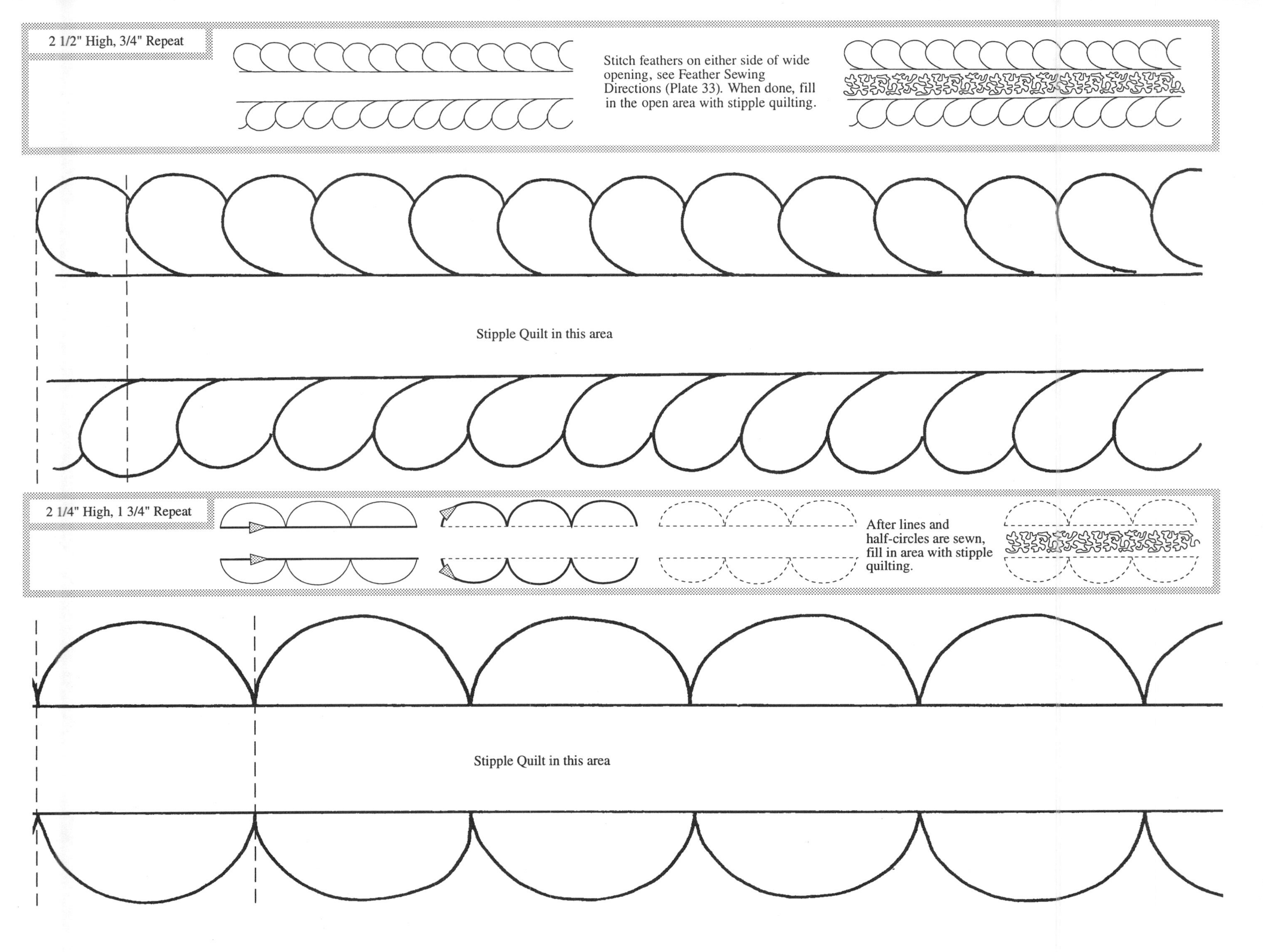
2 1/2" High, 3/4" Repeat
Stitch feathers on either side of wide opening, see Feather Sewing Directions (Plate 33). When done, fill in the open area with stipple quilting.
Stipple Quilt in this area
2 1/4" High, 1 3/4" Repeat
After lines and half-circles are sewn, fill in area with stipple quilting.
Stipple Quilt in this area

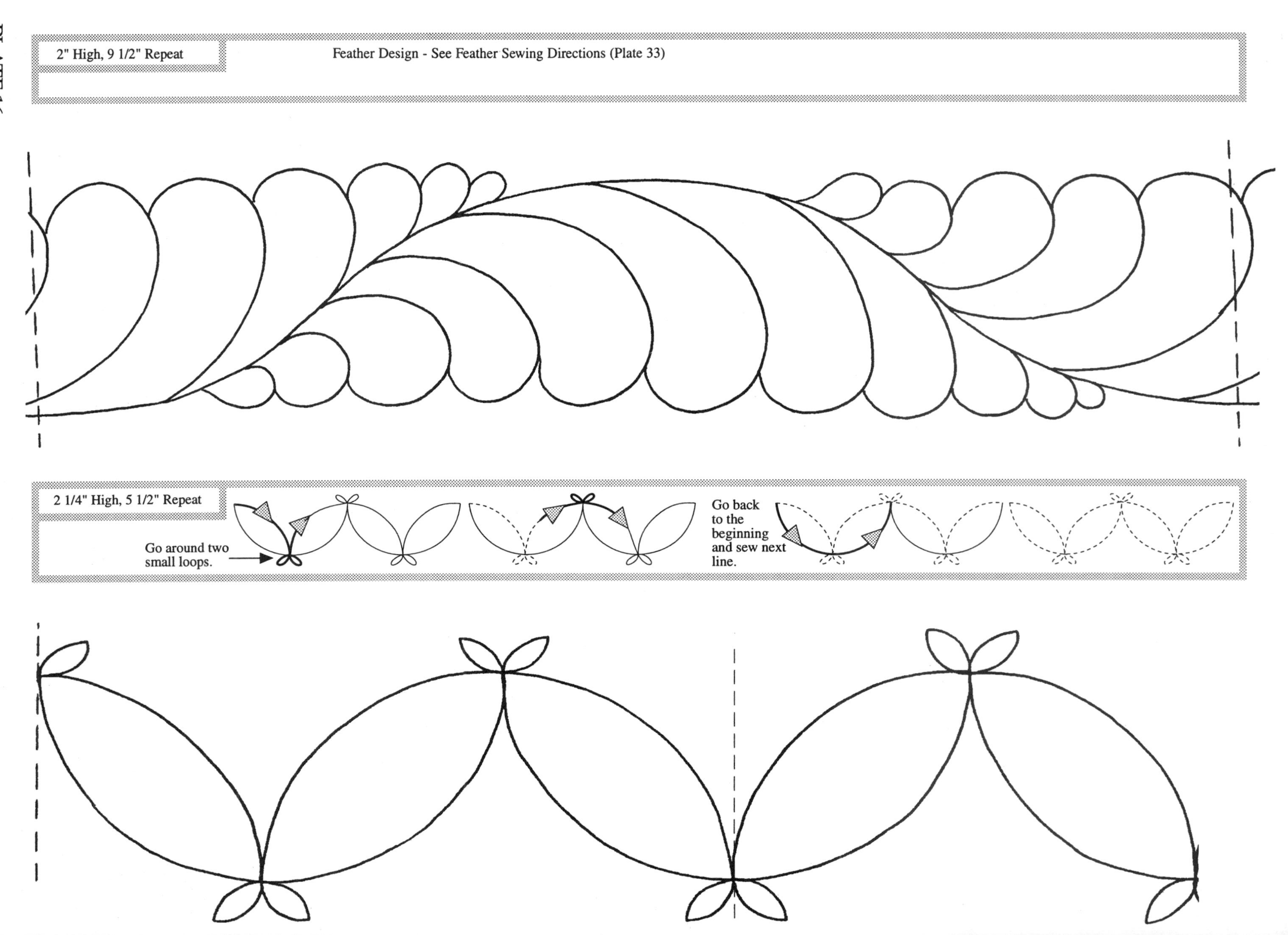

2" High, 9 1/2" Repeat
Feather Design - See Feather Sewing Directions (Plate 33)
2 1/4" High, 5 1/2" Repeat
Go around two small loops.
Go back to the beginning and sew next line.

PLATE 16

2" High, 2 1/4" Repeat
Stitch top of hearts first.
Go back and stitch bottom of hearts
2 1/4" High, 2" Repeat
Stitch top side of hearts first, then go back and stitch the bottom side..

1 1/2" High, 1 1/4" Repeat
Stitch leaves, go up stem and stitch around flower. Go back down stem and stitch next flower.
2" High, 7 1/2" Repeat

PLATE 18

2" High, 2" Repeat
3" High, 1 1/2" Repeat
Start with top row of loops.
Do row of half-circles to form top of heart.
Last, do bottom row of loops.

PLATE 19

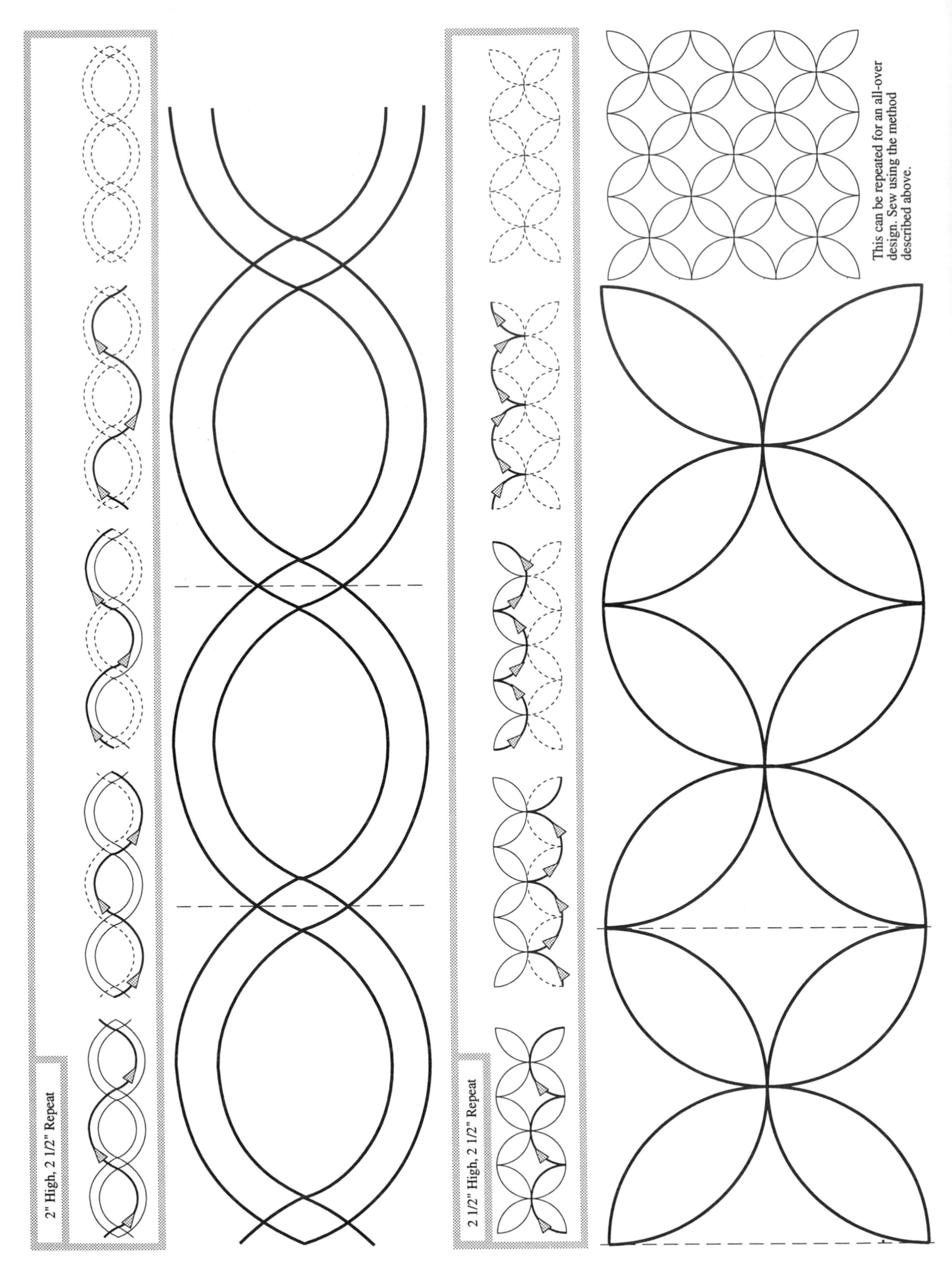

2" High, 2 1/2" Repeat

2 1/2" High, 2 1/2" Repeat

This can be repeated for an all-over design. Sew using the method described above.

PLATE 20

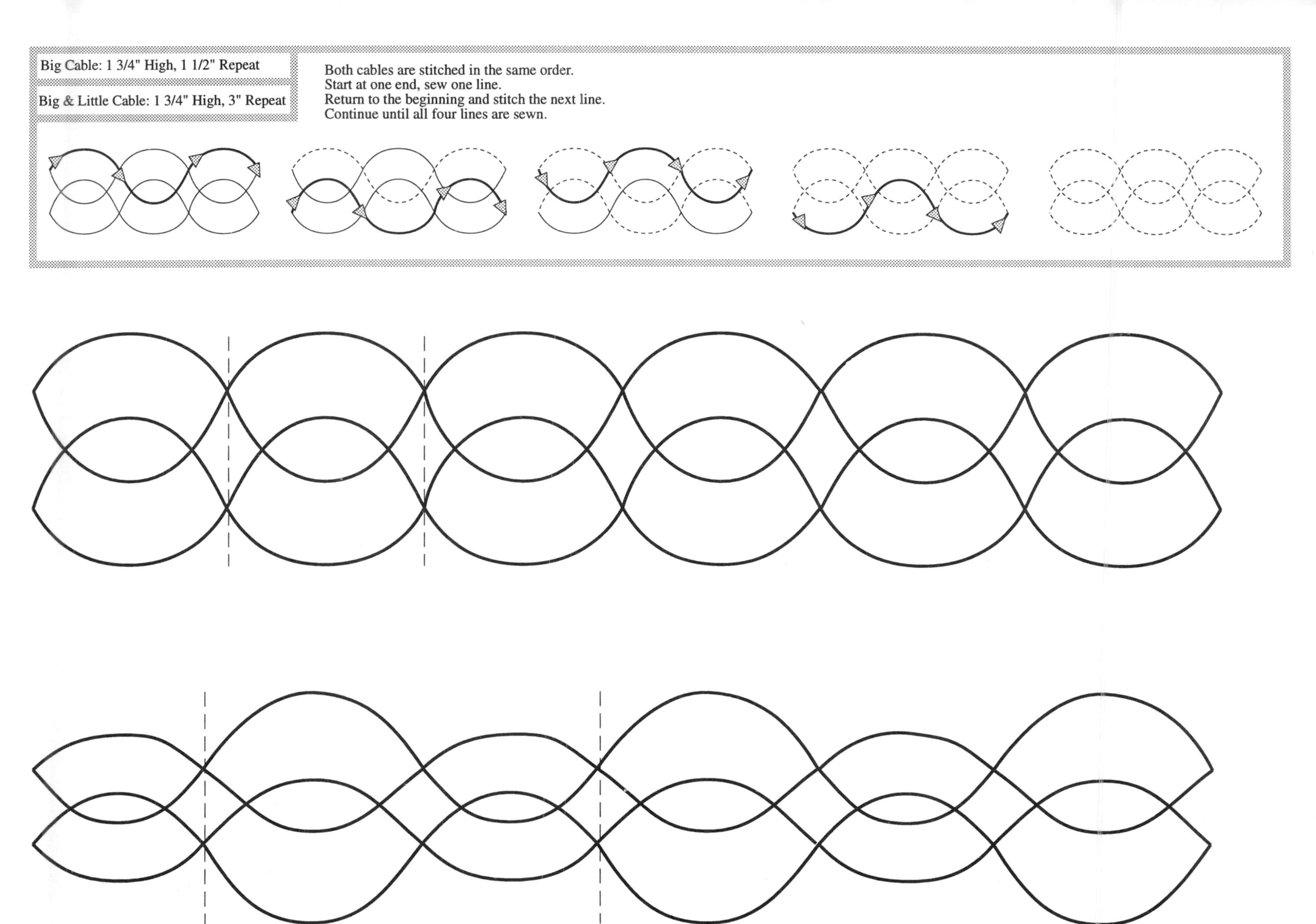
Big Cable: 1 3/4" High, 1 1/2" Repeat
Big & Little Cable: 1 3/4" High, 3" Repeat
Both cables are stitched in the same order.
Start at one end, sew one line.
Return to the beginning and stitch the next line.
Continue until all four lines are sewn.

PLATE 21

PLATE 22

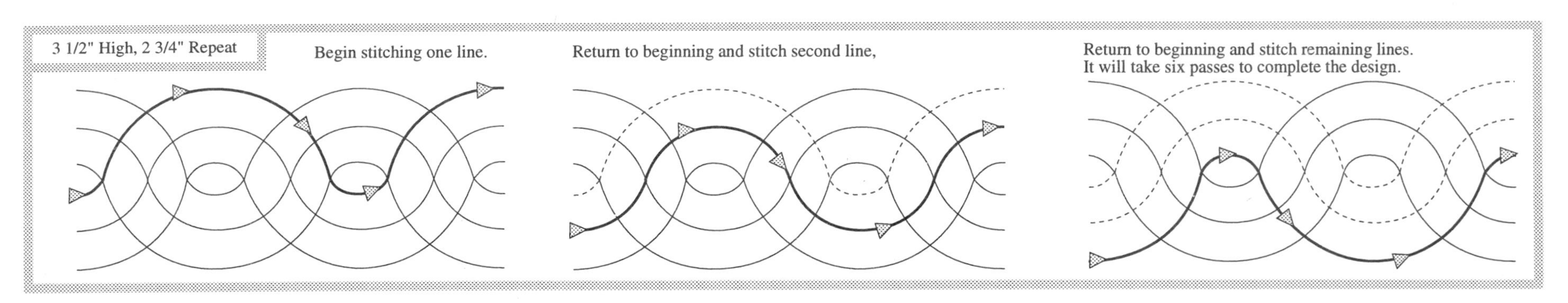

3 1/2" High, 2 3/4" Repeat
Begin stitching one line.
Return to beginning and stitch second line,
Return to beginning and stitch remaining lines.
It will take six passes to complete the design.

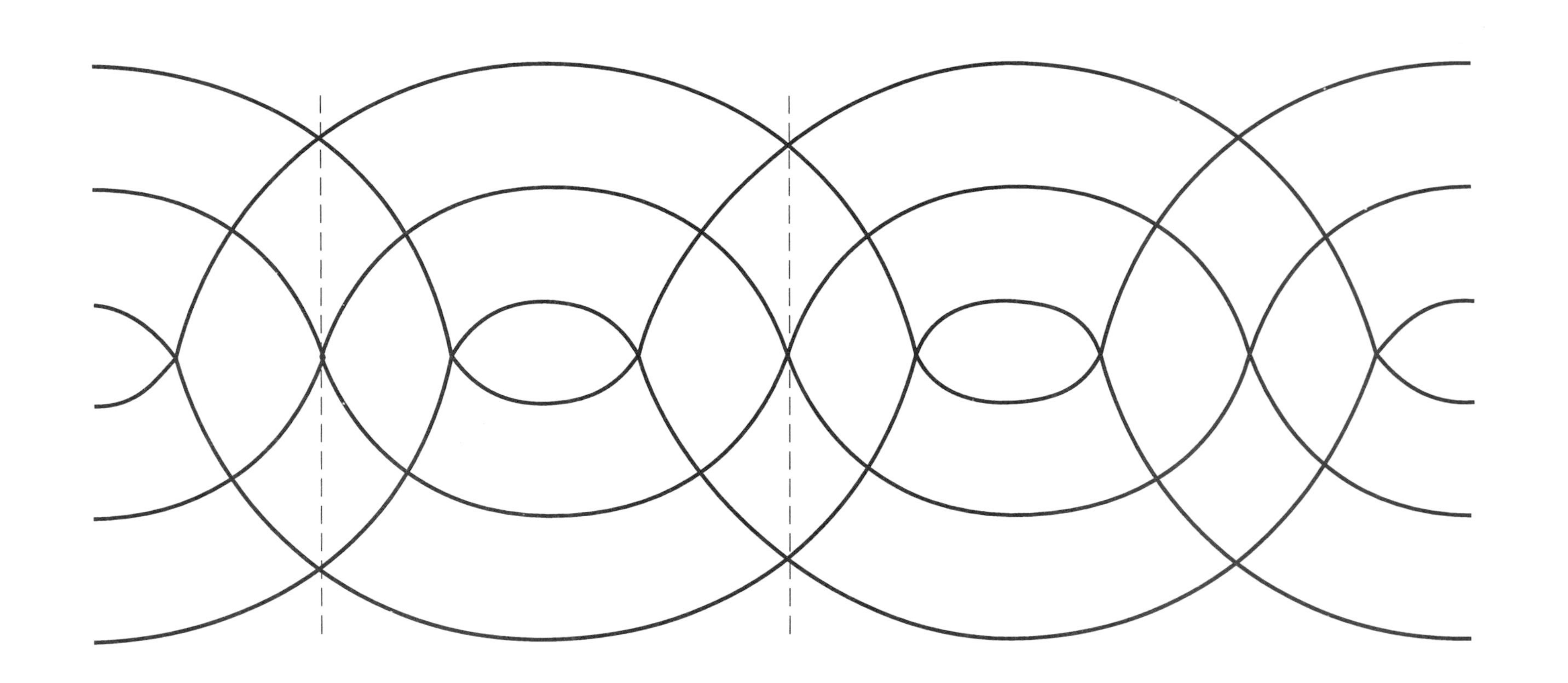

PLATE 23

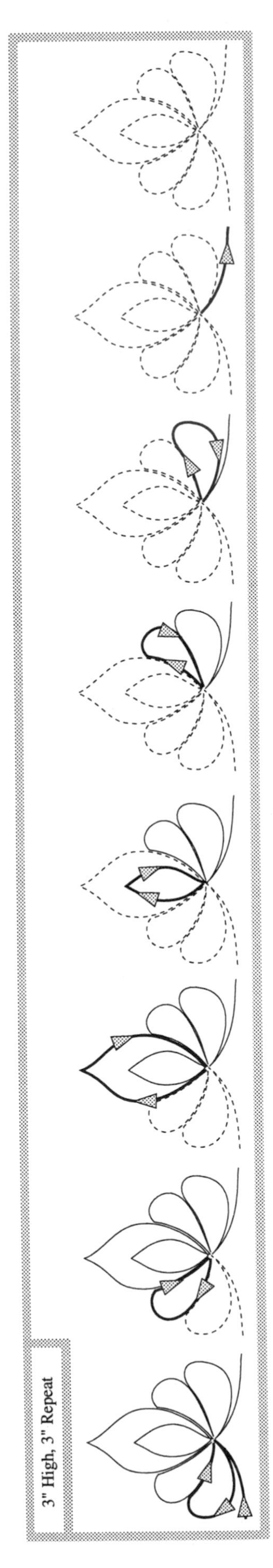
3" High, 3" Repeat

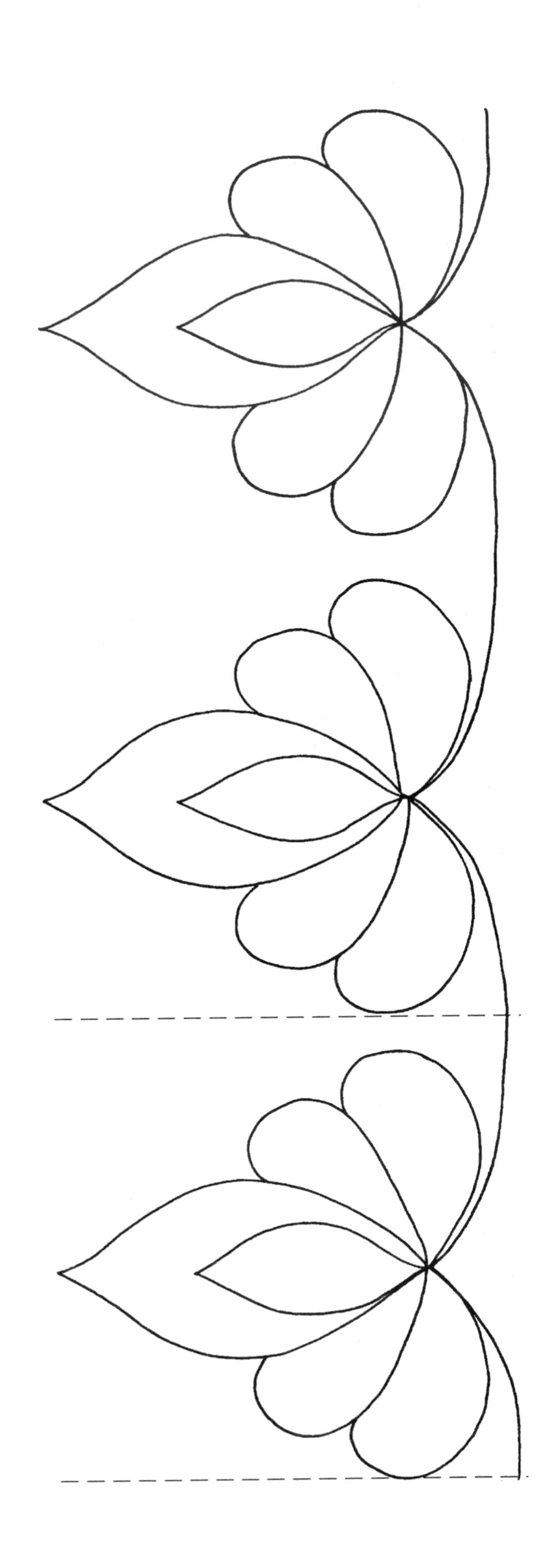

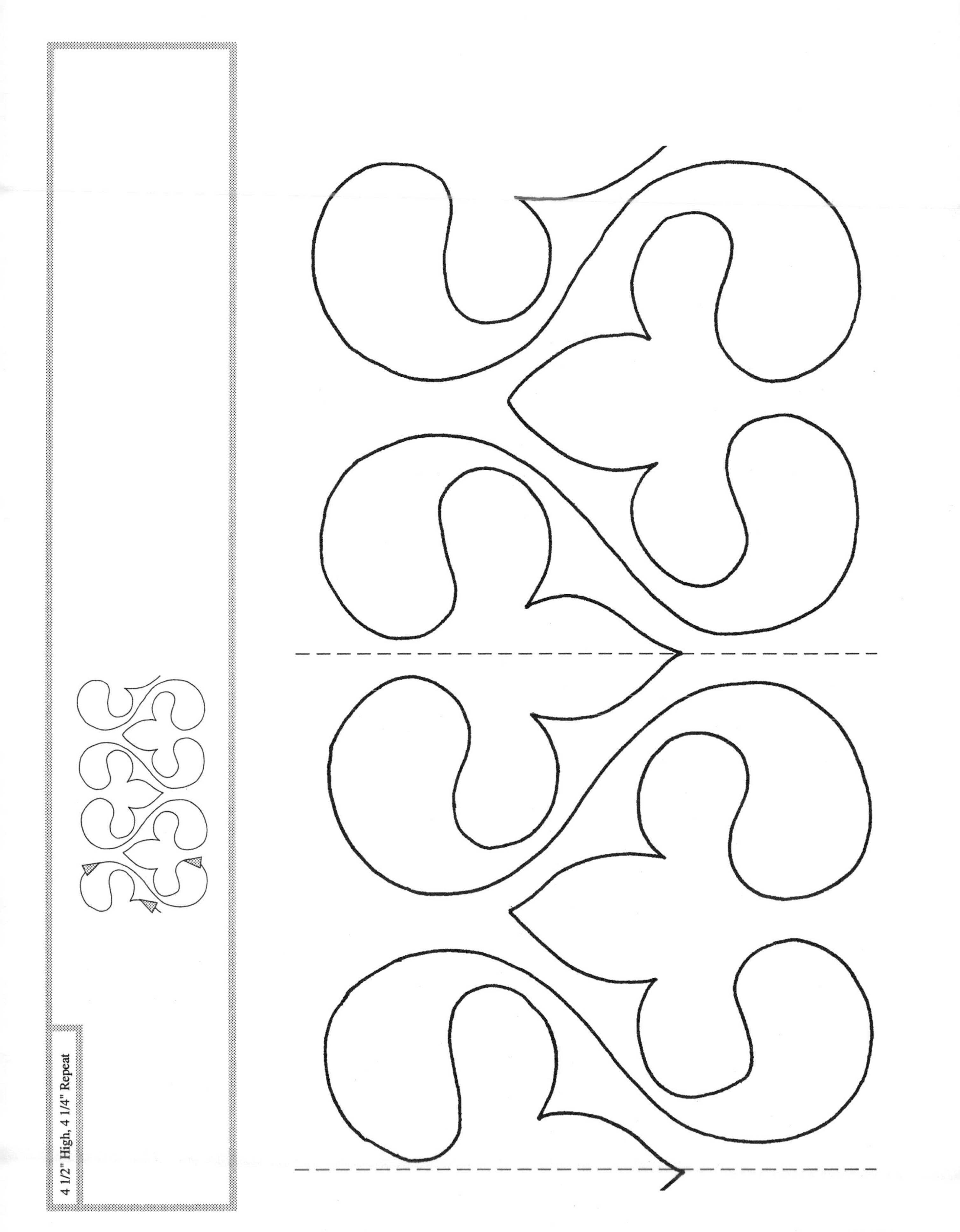

PLATE 25

PLATE 26

PLATE 27

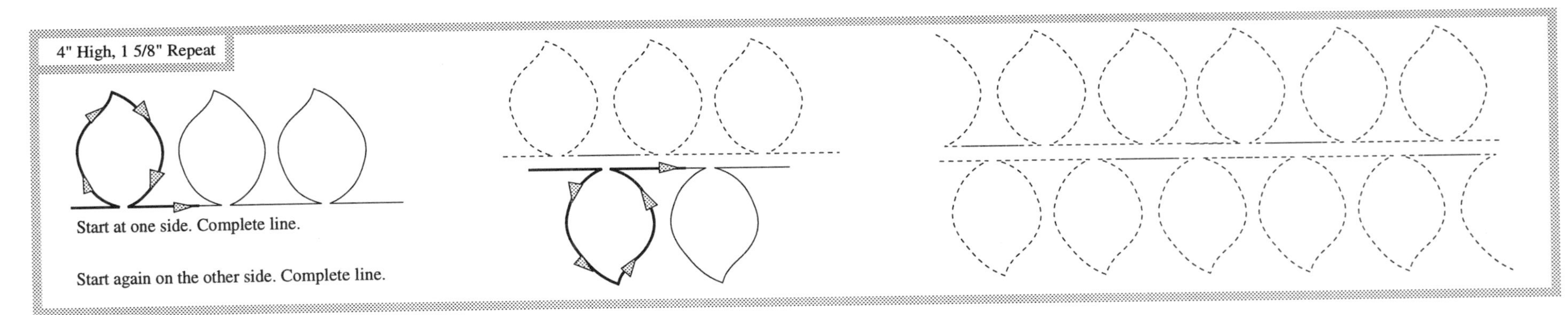
4" High, 1 5/8" Repeat
Start at one side. Complete line.
Start again on the other side. Complete line.

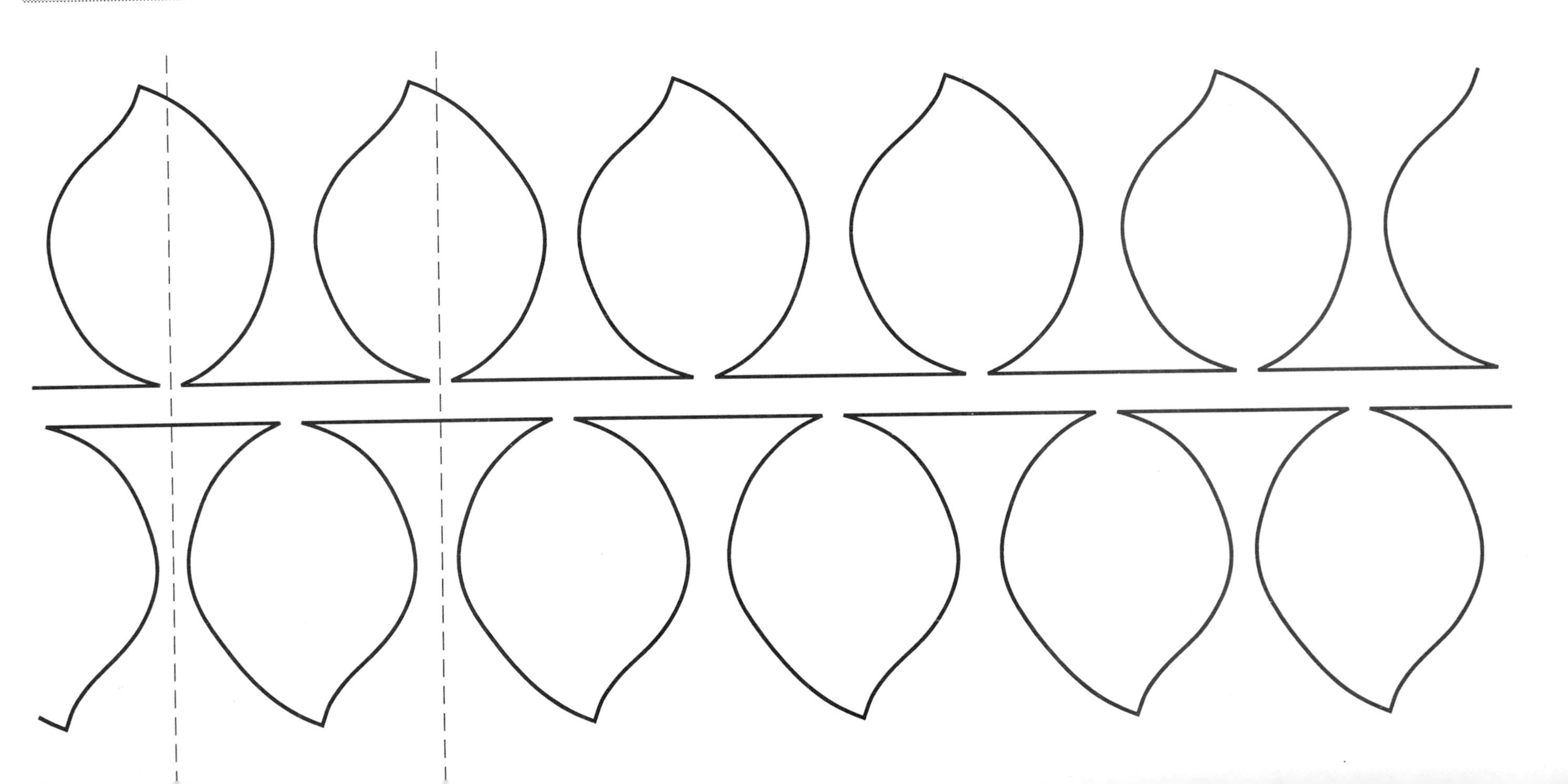

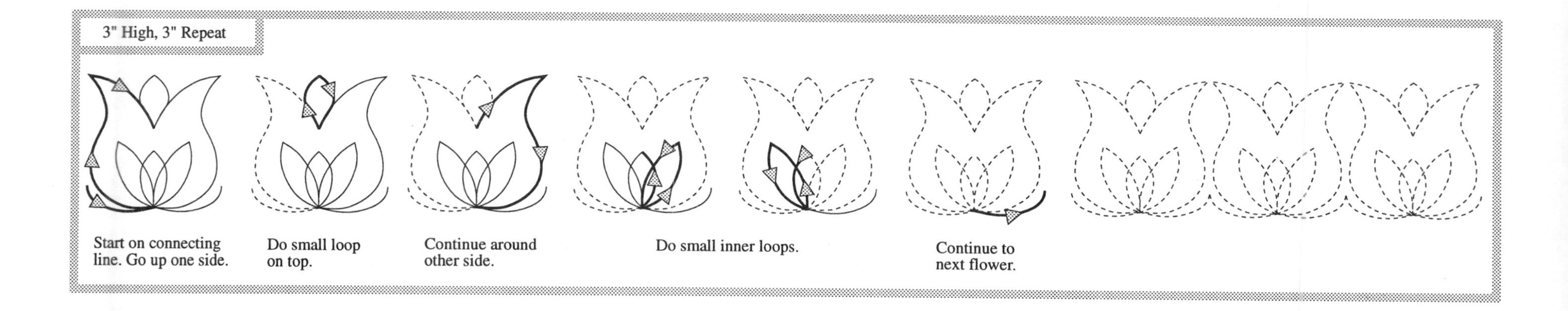
3" High, 3" Repeat
Start on connecting line. Go up one side.
Do small loop on top.
Continue around other side.
Do small inner loops.
Continue to next flower.

4 3/4" High, 9 1/2" Repeat
Stitch along spine.
Sew outer loop first,
then stitch inner loop.
Stitch along spine until
you come to the next loop.
When you complete one side,
go back to the beginning and
sew the other side.

PLATE 30

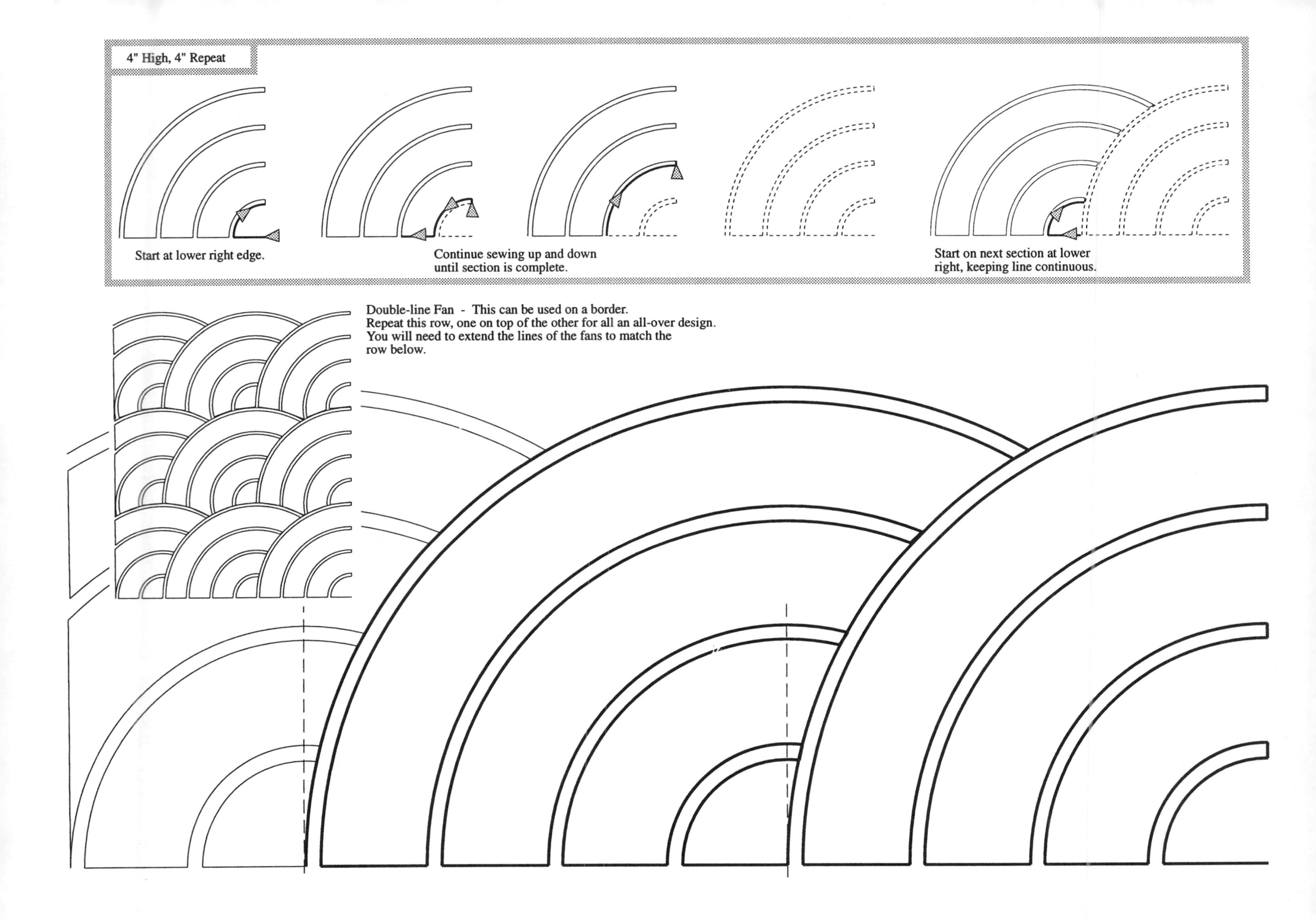
4" High, 4" Repeat
Start at lower right edge.
Continue sewing up and down until section is complete.
Start on next section at lower right, keeping line continuous.
Double-line Fan - This can be used on a border.
Repeat this row, one on top of the other for all an all-over design.
You will need to extend the lines of the fans to match the row below.

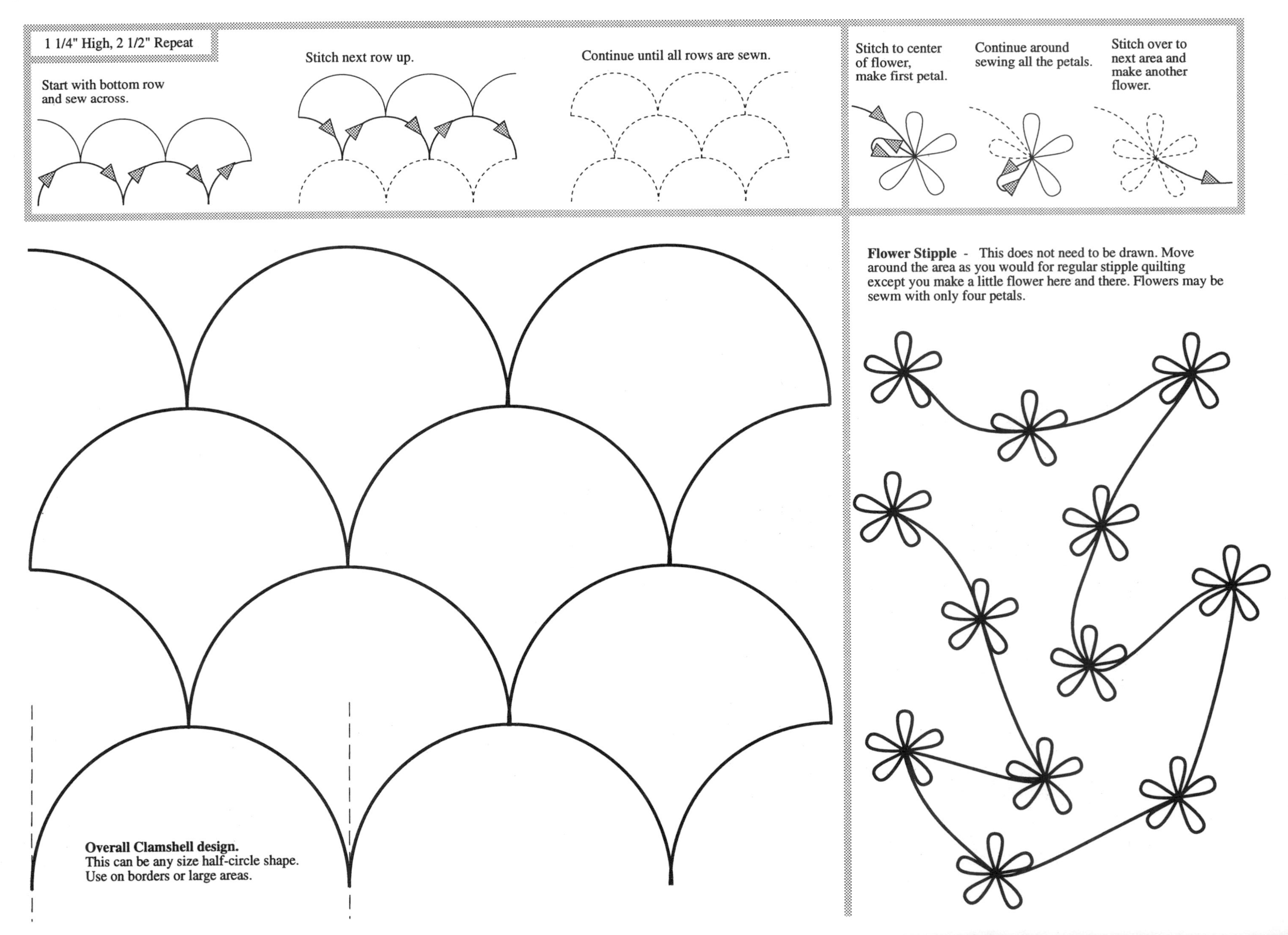

Flower Stipple - This does not need to be drawn. Move around the area as you would for regular stipple quilting except you make a little flower here and there. Flowers may be sewm with only four petals.

Overall Clamshell design.
This can be any size half-circle shape.
Use on borders or large areas.

Feather Sewing Directions

Sew center line (spine) first. Some feather designs have no center line so start with the feathers.

Go back to the start. Begin stitching first feather at the center spine line. Sew around the feather and down along the top part of the next feather.

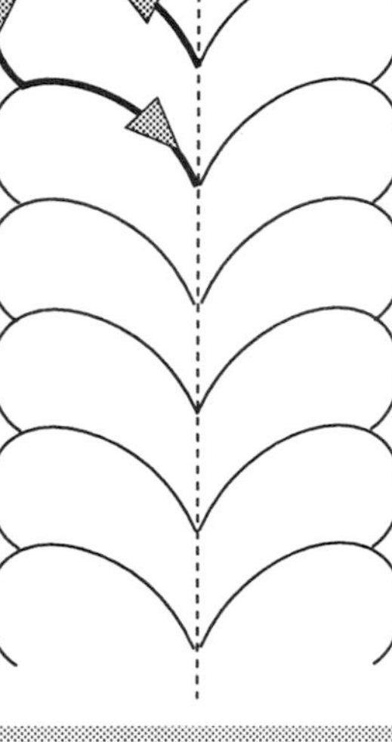

Stitch the second feather by sewing as close as possible back up along the line you have already sewn. Complete the feather by sewing along the top part of the next feather until you reach the spine.

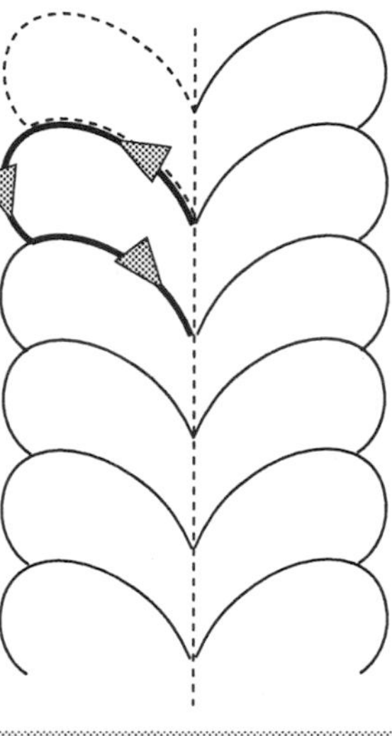

Repeat until all the feathers on one side of the center spine are sewn.

Return to starting point and start sewing feathers on the other side of the center spine.

Continue stitching feathers until the second side is complete.

The drawing shows a double line of quilting stitches between feathers. Your quilting should be as close as possible to the same line and ideally could be one single line. The double row is exaggerated to help show how to stitch.

7 1/2" Square
Feather Design - see Feather Sewing Directions
Start at bottom of small heart.
Stitch around heart and loop.
Sew large heart. Stitch outer
feathers then inner feathers.

6" Square
Start along small circle.
Stitch up and around loop.
Sew back along large loop
and sew feathers as
described in Feather Sewing
Directions
Sew up along other side of loop. Come back down to
first feather and sew. Stitch along small circle to reach
next branch of feathers.

PLATE 35

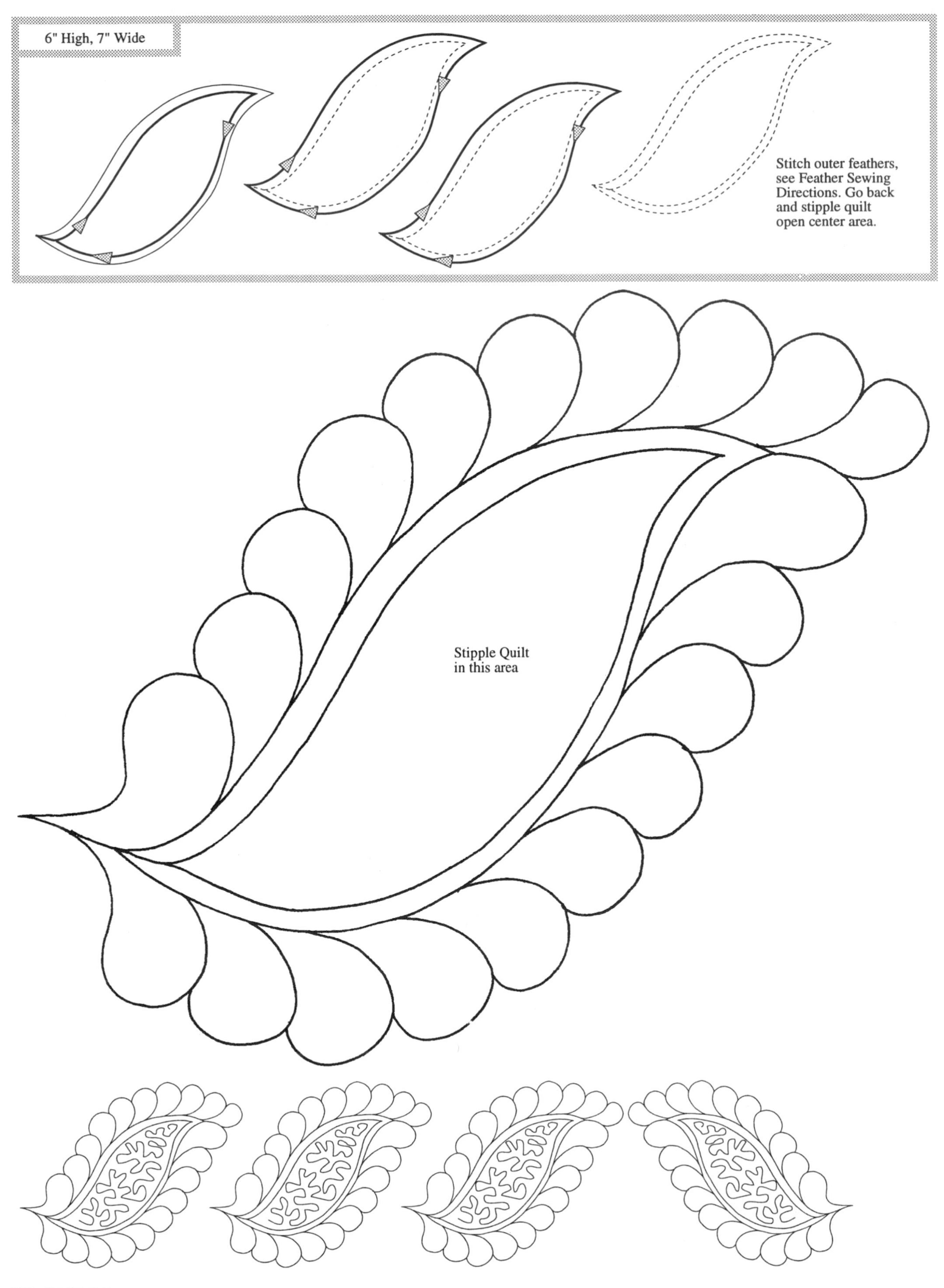

6" High, 7" Wide
Stitch outer feathers, see Feather Sewing Directions. Go back and stipple quilt open center area.
Stipple Quilt in this area

2 1/2" High, 7 1/2" Repeat	1 3/4" High, 6" Repeat	2" High, 7 1/4" Repeat
Feather Designs - See Feather Sewing Directions		After sewing spine and feathers, stitch outer row on both sides.

5" High, 9" Wide
Feather Design - See Feather Sewing Directions

4 1/2" High, 9" Repeat
Feather Design - See Feather Sewing Directions

PLATE 39

5" High, 9 1/2" Repeat
Feather Design - See Feather Sewing Directions

PLATE 40

4 3/4" High, 9 1/2" Repeat
Feather Design - See Feather Sewing Directions
Note there is no central spine. Start at top and sew
one side of feathers then return and sew the other side.

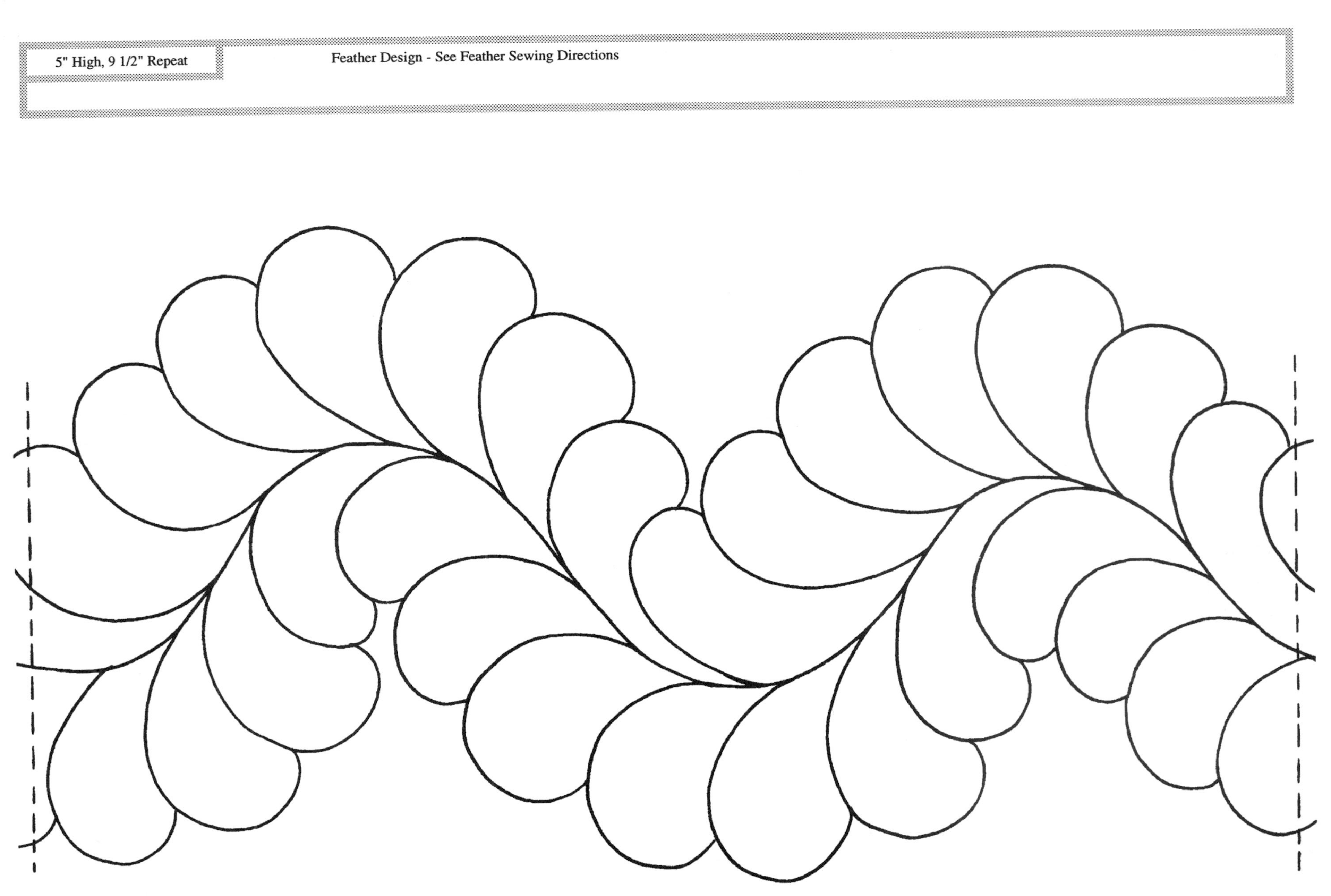
5" High, 9 1/2" Repeat
Feather Design - See Feather Sewing Directions

PLATE 42

5 1/2" High, 9 1/2" Wide

Feather Design - See Feather Sewing Directions
Note there is no central spine to sew. Start sewing at bottom point * and follow line around.

Try reversing the design and using it to fill in a large area or a border.

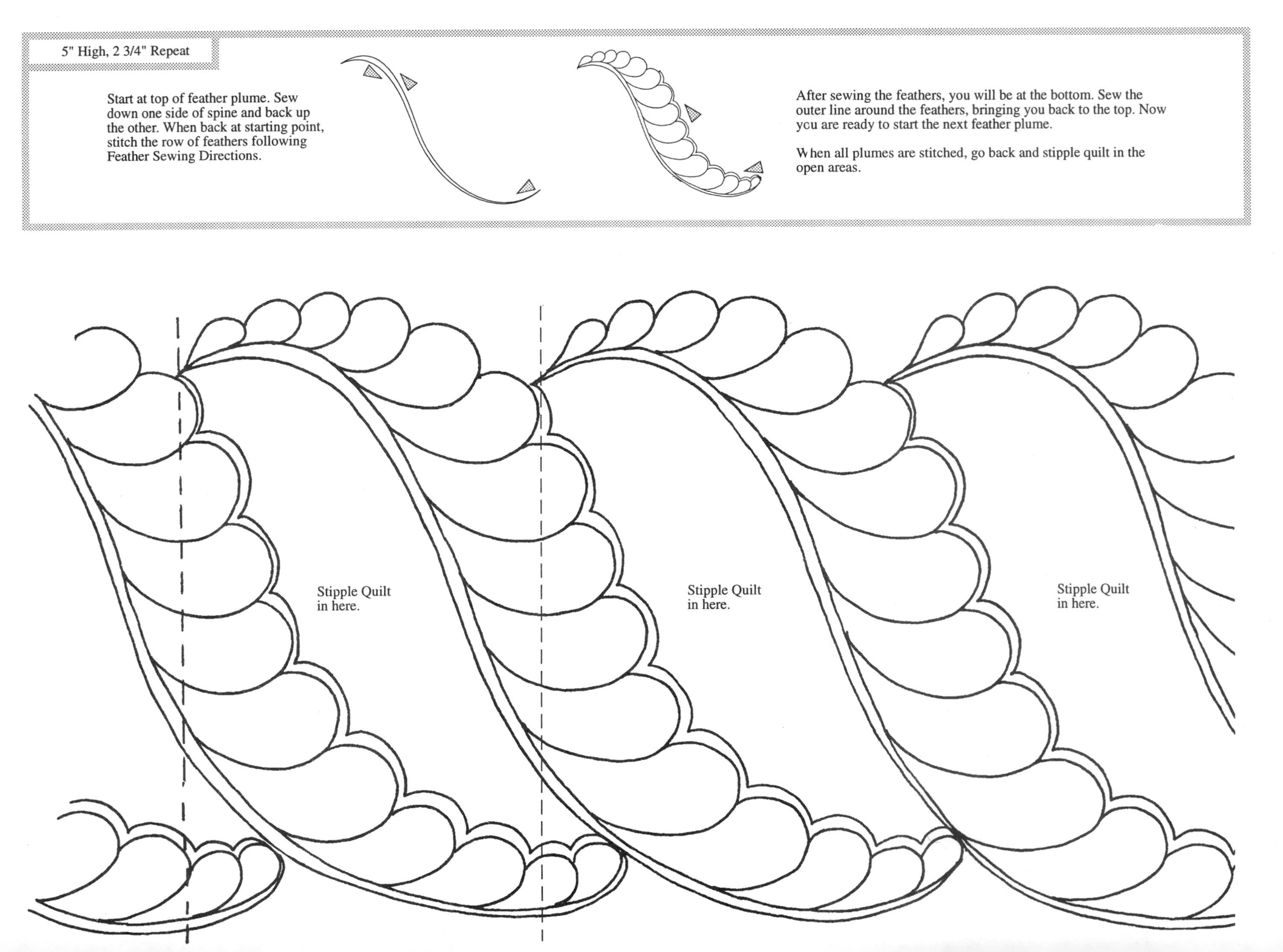
5" High, 2 3/4" Repeat
Start at top of feather plume. Sew down one side of spine and back up the other. When back at starting point, stitch the row of feathers following Feather Sewing Directions.
After sewing the feathers, you will be at the bottom. Sew the outer line around the feathers, bringing you back to the top. Now you are ready to start the next feather plume.
When all plumes are stitched, go back and stipple quilt in the open areas.
Stipple Quilt in here.
Stipple Quilt in here.
Stipple Quilt in here.

PLATE 44